D0012689

MORE PRAISE FOR E.

"Candid. Practical. Empowering. *Helpful. Earn It!* should be required reading for any young professional who wants to be taken seriously and who wants to get ahead."

—**Meg Jay, PhD, author of** *The Defining Decade: Why Your Twenties Matter—And How to Make the Most of Them Now* **and** *Supernormal*

"Read this book! Mika and Daniela provide some of the most solid and straightforward advice that I have read in a long time. The advice in *Earn It!* is priceless and will have you at the top of your game."

—**Rebecca Minkoff**

"Mika and Daniela have written a powerful step-by-step guide chock-full of advice from trailblazing women on how to achieve supreme success and power in any field."

—**André Leon Talley, former contributing editor to** *Vogue*

"No matter where you're at in your career, you'll glean plenty from the lessons and anecdotes in this book. Brzezinski and Pierre-Bravo show readers what resourcefulness and intrepidness look like in the real world, and in doing so, encourage women to be the best versions of their butt-kicking selves."

—**Kristin Wong, author of** *Get Money: Live the Life You Want, Not Just the Life You Can Afford*

Hillsboro Public Library
Hillsboro, OR
A member of Washington County
COOPERATIVE LIBRARY SERVICES

ALSO BY MIKA BRZEZINSKI

*Know Your Value: Women, Money, and Getting What You're
Worth*
Grow Your Value: Living and Working to Your Full Potential
Obsessed: America's Food Addiction—and My Own
All Things at Once

MIKA BRZEZINSKI
WITH DANIELA PIERRE-BRAVO

EARN IT!

Know Your Value and Grow Your Career, in Your 20s and Beyond

hachette
BOOKS

NEW YORK BOSTON

Copyright © 2019 by Mika Brzezinski

Cover design by Carlos Esparza and Amanda Kain
Cover photograph by Miller Hawkins
Cover copyright © 2019 by Hachette Book Group, Inc.

Hachette Book Group supports the right to free expression and the value of copyright. The purpose of copyright is to encourage writers and artists to produce the creative works that enrich our culture.

The scanning, uploading, and distribution of this book without permission is a theft of the author's intellectual property. If you would like permission to use material from the book (other than for review purposes), please contact permissions@hbgusa.com. Thank you for your support of the author's rights.

Hachette Books
Hachette Book Group
1290 Avenue of the Americas
New York, NY 10104
hachettebookgroup.com
twitter.com/hachettebooks

First Edition: May 2019

Hachette Books is a division of Hachette Book Group, Inc.

The Hachette Books name and logo are trademarks of Hachette Book Group, Inc.

The publisher is not responsible for websites (or their content) that are not owned by the publisher.

The Hachette Speakers Bureau provides a wide range of authors for speaking events. To find out more, go to www.hachettespeakersbureau.com or call (866) 376-6591.

Print book interior design by Christine Marra, *Marra*thon Production Services. www.marrathoneditorial.org

Library of Congress Control Number: 2018961991

ISBNs: 978-1-60286-591-4 (trade paperback), 978-1-60286-592-1 (ebook)

Printed in the United States of America

33614081398561

LSC-C

10 9 8 7 6 5 4 3 2 1

For my girls, Emilie and Carlie, Sophie,
Aurora, Katherine, Emilie Garner, Sofia,
Sunny, and all the girls in my life.
This is for you.

CONTENTS

ACKNOWLEDGMENTS

To Amanda Murray, Georgina Levitt—I am so thankful to be able to continue working with you and for your support and vision for this book. Special thanks to Patricia Mulcahy who helped see this through and made sure we got it right.

Andy Lack, Phil Griffin, Steve Burke, Brian Roberts, David Cohen, and everyone in my Comcast NBCUniversal family, including Vicki Neidigh and Shawn Leavitt, for believing in the importance of providing a strong platform for Know Your Value. And thank you, Jared DiPalma, for doing and re-doing the math.

To the entire Know Your Value team, starting with Jane Kaupp, Maureen Clancy, Emily Cassidy, Duby McDowell, Robyn Gengras, Aliyah Frumin, Bianca Brosh, Maria Gronda, Stephen Hoelper, Marcy Ilicich, Terese Guerrero, and Stacey Greenman. You guys rock.

And above all—to my girls. I thank my daughters for inspiring me every day to share this message with other women.

If I've learned one thing in my career, it's the importance of being able to effectively communicate your value. To be able to articulate what you are contributing, which niche you're filling, how the group benefits from your role, and what all of that is worth. This idea of understanding what you bring to the table and being able to communicate it so that you get what you need and deserve—both in your work life and your personal life—is critical for women of all ages.

It's become a passion of mine: I want to help women everywhere learn how to advocate for themselves in real time, and to own their voice and messaging while they do it.

I learned my lessons the hard way. I wrote about my own struggle to be paid fairly at work in my book *Know Your Value: Women, Money, and Getting What You're Worth*. I wrote it because I wanted to explore effective strategies: How can women get the money they deserve and the promotions they want? How can they best accelerate their career opportunities and leverage their talents without provoking a backlash or being counterproductive? I learned that, bottom line, women don't negotiate enough, and when they do, they don't necessarily do it productively. Women can't advocate for themselves in precisely the same way men do—it doesn't work. As we navigate gender bias, we confront different dynamics in getting ahead.

In my book I shared my vulnerabilities and shortcomings when it came time to go to the negotiating table. I shared what *not to do*. But I also explained which strategies ultimately worked for me. In the end, I closed my gender wage gap by refusing to play the victim or apologize. I was ready to walk. Most important, I learned to communicate my professional value.

My story clearly struck a chord. Hundreds of women started coming up to me—in airports, at industry events, and on the street—to tell me how my story helped them get raises, and ultimately gave them the tools to empower their own voices. I am so proud of all the women who have taken this message and applied it to their own lives. Now they're not only claiming higher paychecks, but also recognition and the rewards that come with it.

I may have jump-started an important discussion, but the work didn't end there. Over the past few years, what started as a book has evolved into the Know Your Value movement—a conference series and multiplatform digital hub that continues to give women the tools to develop and inspire their individual growth.

But as I look back at my own career path and the ideas we talk about in my conference series, it dawns on me that the demands and pressures on women in their 20s are different now. Young women in the workplace, whether starting out or making important next steps to further their careers, have a whole new set of challenges and circumstances that make realizing their professional ambitions both exciting and difficult. They are navigating a different terrain than the one traveled by women of my generation.

While many of the lessons in *Know Your Value* are still relevant—communicating what you bring to the table effectively to get paid what you are worth; advocating for yourself in the moment—there are a few lessons that need to be added for women in the early stages of their careers.

In some ways, younger women have more going for them than I did in my 20s. The workplace is ripe with opportunity for women to succeed and get ahead. They are entering male-dominated fields in greater numbers than ever before, although some fields show greater progress than others.

Yet young women still face a familiar set of challenges: in addition to gender bias that's an everyday occurrence in the corporate world, they are often dismissed because of their youth. Millennial women in particular get a bad rap, accused of being part of a generation that is distracted, entitled, and lazy. They're encouraged to present themselves as self-assured and ambitious, but not overly aggressive, which would make them less likeable (and God forbid a woman is labeled as "difficult"!). These are contradictory messages for women who are entering the work-place and don't understand the office environment. And then there are our own tendencies, as women, to overthink situations and take things personally.

An incident involving my former assistant brought the stereo-type into sharp focus for me.

Sitting in my office during a half-hour break from cohosting *Morning Joe,* I scarfed down some oatmeal and fruit before getting ready for a short interview. Even eating is a scheduled part of my morning; that particular day was otherwise swamped with meetings, conference calls, and evening events.

André Leon Talley, the well-known fashion editor, had graciously agreed to stop by my office early that morning for a recorded interview to be used in my 2015 book, *Grow Your Value.* A friend and frequent contributor to my Know Your Value conferences and books, André always offers honest advice on how to get ahead in the workplace.

Emily, my then assistant, was assigned to coordinate the interview with André, and to assist me at my scheduled events for the rest of the day. The plan was for me to do the interview with André, go back and finish the show, and then leave with Emily for Philadelphia, where I was to deliver an 11:30 a.m. speech in front of 500 women on the topic of equal pay. The timing was tight, as usual: we all had to keep moving and make it work. For the people who assist me, there is little room for error.

I lean heavily on efficient assistants like Emily to help keep the details of my life and work on track. In our early days together, she worked primarily out of my home office, a much more relaxed and casual setup than the *Morning Joe* offices in Manhattan. I'm usually in sweats at home, so I suggested to Emily that she should feel free to dress casually. I had also forewarned her that the culture at the Rockefeller Center office would be different; on the days we were in the city, she'd have to look professional. But it was on Emily to figure out that balance between professionalism and comfort—I didn't think to give her clear guidelines.

The André Leon Talley interview took place during one of her first workdays at 30 Rock. He arrived in my office that day draped in a gorgeous maroon cape, with Emily in tow. As we sat down, I saw André's brow furrow; he looked uncomfortable. He was watching Emily as she zipped from one side of the room to the other, setting up the interview. I could tell something about my assistant didn't sit well with him.

Emily had come in on a pair of four-inch heels I'd given her a long time ago—heels I'd decided were ridiculously high on me but might be fun for a younger person to wear on a night out, or even on a date. That day she wore them in the office, along with a flashy dress. Her hair, usually up in a ponytail, was blown out to full volume.

The interview room was very small. I realized that Emily, with her perfume, her hair, her high heels, and her movements, seemed to take up the whole room. She kept interrupting us inadvertently by moving animatedly around the room, wearing a smile from ear to ear, her heels clicking from one side to the other. Once or twice, she reached in between André and me; she didn't have much sense of personal space.

I finally told her André and I could do the interview alone: she had set herself up right beside us, as if the meeting were for the three of us. I'm sure she thought by staying in the room she was being helpful, but when you're working as an assistant and a high-level person comes in, less is more. It would have been more appropriate for her to have asked me beforehand, "Do you want me in here for this interview?"

I knew her intentions were good. This was a young woman whom I was training, grooming, and mentoring professionally. And yet I found myself wondering, "What's wrong with me, that I'm so impeded by her presence?"

Once Emily left the room, we started to roll tape. André and I approached the subject of working, training, and identifying talent. Although sometimes too candid, André always offers insightful advice. To prove a point, he used Emily, whom he'd just met, to illustrate his point about young people entering the workforce. "She does not know her place. She's all over the place. She thinks it's all about her."

I would never use those words to describe Emily. She had already worked for me for several years and had proven herself to be trustworthy, hardworking, and very dedicated to the details of her work. And she was equally dedicated to the details of working with me and my family. She never balked at any of the sometimes-crazy tasks I assigned her and had always seemed grateful for the opportunities her job presented her. She had shown nothing but loyalty, kindness, and eagerness.

André's comments really threw me off. I told him: "Actually, she was a teacher in Philadelphia and is now my assistant. I really love her. She's a wonderful girl." I was completely taken aback.

"It doesn't come off that way to me at all. It's her demeanor—it's all wrong." To him, André explained, her behavior read *entitled*.

I didn't think about it too much, but as the day went on

I started noticing things about Emily that I hadn't seen before. We had a rough trip to Philadelphia that day after the interview: it was a disaster. We were very rushed to get to the speech. She didn't have a notepad for me in the car, so we had to stop and buy one, and were delayed twenty minutes. As I ran to the stage, Emily could barely keep up in those heels.

I let the details of that day go and just put the whole thing to the back of my mind. I really adored Emily. She had been such an asset to keeping my home and work–life balance in check—and all the chaos that came with it—that I wanted to continue working on her professionally. I wanted to see her succeed. I was still processing.

The next day, I came home from the show to find a despondent version of my normally bubbly assistant waiting for me in my home office. She was apprehensive, and worried, and looked like someone who'd just been told she was fired.

"Do you think I'm entitled?" she asked me hesitantly, her eyes glistening.

It turned out that the tape of my interview with André had turned up on her desk to be transcribed. How could I think that wouldn't happen?

Hearing those negative comments about herself firsthand was clearly a gut-punch that had rocked Emily to her core. But ultimately, as we dissected the feedback, the experience proved to be an important turning point in her budding career.

Talking with Emily that day was also clarifying for me. I had new perspective on what it means to be a young woman today who wants to succeed, reach her career goals, and advocate for herself, but whose messaging is off—and she doesn't even know it. While Emily might have thought she was projecting confidence and self-assurance, her audience wasn't receiving the same message. What was causing the disconnect?

People use the word "entitled" to describe someone who seems to feel they inherently deserve something. But isn't that also the basis of ambition—that innate desire for, and expectation of, success? And isn't being ambitious and self-assured a good thing? It absolutely is.

Clearly there's a disconnect and a double standard in how we expect young women to show their ambition. The challenge is to understand the playing field you're working on, and to minimize the internal voices that get in the way of your ability to develop professionally.

How can you be fully comfortable and exert confidence and self-assurance if someone can mistake that as looking entitled? How can you be self-aware enough to disprove the stereotypes, but have enough confidence to advocate for yourself when it's time to grow in your career? It comes down to how you show your ambition. In the workplace, there is absolutely room for ambitious women to find a place and move on, once you figure out the office etiquette and the protocols already in place.

I'm a daughter of a former national security advisor and an artist. I went to the best colleges. And I've always tried to be self-deprecating because I worried I would appear entitled. I grew up with children of presidents; I understand what entitled looks like. And Emily was not that, not at all.

Even at the age of 24, Emily was incredibly hardworking, and had done everything and anything that was ever asked of her. She was not raised to think of herself as deserving special privileges. She went to Penn State and worked as a teacher in a tough school district in South Philadelphia before working for me. She comes from a fantastic family of teachers and has amazing parents who are kind and so loving. They're absolutely wonderful. Their unconditional support led her to believe that the world at large would welcome her just as warmly; but in the workplace, that's just not how it goes. Unconditional love stops at the front door.

While it was a tough experience, Emily learned a lot from that day and has made great strides on her long-term career journey. She has contributed to books on women's issues, written articles for the Know Your Value website, and transferred into a new role as manager of sales enablement on the business side of Know Your Value. In her role she executes the brand's social and digital strategy and helps to oversee high-profile national events. She's someone I trust and rely on completely both as a professional and a friend.

But she needed that really rough day to get a jump-start. Emily today is a very different person from the young woman you just read about. She has developed self-assurance and poise, she knows her value, and she's learned to translate that into a good salary and a solid reputation. Plus, she's fun, self-aware, and confident enough to let us tell this story as the opening of this book. That, I say, is a winner.

This story isn't just about wearing the right outfit or the right shoes. It's about owning your presence and your voice, learning to read your audience, and figuring out how to use that to your advantage. What other special hurdles do twenty-something women face in learning their value, asking for it, and getting it—and most important, how do they overcome those hurdles?

My goal with this book is to share real lessons about the struggle that young women face today as they try to show their ambition and develop their careers.

I see so many young women who are smart, eager, energetic, and determined to get ahead. They feel a sense of urgency to get to the top and become successful from the get-go. Young women worry about losing time if they don't pick the "perfect job" right away, fearful that with so many choices, making the wrong one might lead them down the wrong career path entirely. By the time they reach their mid-20s, many are paralyzed by choice overload, and the pressure to succeed.

I want young women to examine and develop their self-worth from the start of their careers, understand their power as women, and learn to use the many tools at their disposal to build a strong professional persona. We'll go over the many ways you can own your ambition, not shy away from it.

I'll try and answer questions such as: How can I manage the obstacles in front of me when getting started in my career? How can I become an asset to my workplace? How can I stand out in the beginning of my career if I'm not the one calling the shots? How can I grow effectively and advocate for myself when the time is right? And how will I know when to stick it out through a tough work environment, as opposed to when to know when it's time to jump ship and perhaps strike out on my own?"

For this book I decided to team up with a talented young woman on our *Morning Joe* team, my coauthor, Daniela Pierre-Bravo, to collaborate and explore the crossroads faced by women in their 20s.

You'll hear her story, along with the stories of other highly successful women and men, from Hollywood to politics to business. They'll share their stories of failures and successes, how they found their voices and navigated the workplace to their advantage, and what they advise for the next generation. You'll also hear additional voices from young women who have paved their paths in their own way, from successful young executives who have climbed the corporate ladder to a recent grad who developed her own company in college to millennial women who started in traditional corporate jobs and decided after a while to be their own boss.

We'll dig deep into the things that get in the way of embracing and owning your voice—from our society's dependency on technology to feeling lost and anxious about that next step.

We'll share our research collaboration with Harvard University's Institute of Politics (IOP), and the insights from focus groups and polls that were created exclusively for this book. We'll get to the "why" behind the questions and then offer solutions.

The future of the workplace is for young women to define. I want young women entering the workforce to understand and be able to communicate their value right out of the gate. To build their own narrative and communicate confidently who they are and what they bring to the table.

There are so many ways to bring out your effective, strong,

confident, determined, ambitious self. With the help of my millennial coauthor, who knows what your generation is up against firsthand, and many others who have contributed their expertise and advice to this book, I'll show you the tools you need to act on the strength of your convictions and move ahead in the workplace and beyond.

CHAPTER ONE

DANIELA'S STORY

Applause erupted from the audience as we wrapped *Morning Joe*'s three-hour live show in Charleston, South Carolina, the first of three days of broadcasting from an important primary state that would help define the presidential election of 2016.

Less than an hour from the end of the program, I was already racing out the door to catch a jet to Chattanooga, Tennessee, to give an afternoon speech at a women's conference. I had started my day at 3:30 a.m., and by 10 a.m. the adrenaline from being on the show was beginning to fade. I was exhausted. Staffing me that day was a young producer from *Morning Joe*, Daniela Pierre-Bravo.

Originally, I had planned to have another staffer join me on the trip, but she fell ill at the last minute. As a replacement, the first person I thought of was Daniela. I knew I could count on her for everything from getting my coffee right to bigger tasks like booking a major newsmaker on *Morning Joe*.

As one of the show's producers, she was the first person on set that morning, a 4 a.m. call time. Staffing me that day meant she would travel with me to Tennessee and back that night to South Carolina to do the show from there all over again the next morning. She was just as exhausted as I was, but you wouldn't

1

know it from the way she handled herself. She was always on and ready to work.

At that point, I had known her for two years, first as an NBC page.

The day we met, she got a quick introduction to the daily chaos behind the scenes on *Morning Joe*. I was in the middle of a typically hectic morning, racing to get ready to go on air. Interns scuttled around in a frenzy, looking for a scarf to match my outfit that day—minutes before showtime.

As my makeup artist dusted my face with powder, I welcomed this eager-looking newcomer before she could get in a word of greeting. After she indicated how glad she was to be part of our team, amid the hustle and bustle I asked if she would be the one getting my coffee in the morning.

"Yes!" she exclaimed proudly.

"Good!" I said, only half-kidding. "You better not f*** it up!"

Laughter filled the room, but she could tell I meant it.

Daniela remembers the moment well: "Though I knew Mika was joking, her comment also shook me: clearly I had an opportunity to gain her trust, and to stand out, even just by getting her coffee right."

Because I work around the clock, often late into the night, and get wake-up calls at 3 a.m. every weekday to cohost a three- or sometimes four-hour live show without breaks, trust me, that coffee will either MAKE OR BREAK ME. I NEED it to get me through the early mornings.

Daniela quickly intuited that it was the lifeline to my day: "The details of that critical order—venti black-eye misto, extra hot, extra foam—rang in my head every morning," she recalls. "The show-day routine was always the same. I would stand outside Starbucks at 4:45 a.m. pleading with the barista to open a few minutes early so Mika could get her order the moment she sat in the makeup chair. I had little face time with Mika back then, so making sure her coffee was done right was crucial!"

And it was! She treated the errand like her life depended on it. And that attitude spilled over to the other parts of her job. I felt assured that whenever she was around, things were going to go smoothly. I found myself making certain to bring her along to whatever event or work commitment I had. She gained my trust initially by making my work life easier.

The next thing she knew, Daniela was accompanying me from fashion shows to offsite shoots. Long days started with her helping me get show-ready when it was still dark out, and often ended after events that went late into the evening. It was a grueling schedule, but she was meeting and interacting with high-profile people from the editor in chief of *Cosmopolitan* to media moguls and CEOs of Fortune 500 companies.

As Daniela puts it: "Mika opened up a world of access. Getting the small details of my job right helped me turn what was meant to be a three-month assignment at *Morning Joe* as an NBC page into a full-time job in less than a month and a half."

As the show's production coordinator, she ran point in the studio, zipping between the greenrooms to the set at a mile a minute, prepping guests, and putting out fires. After a quick stop as an associate producer, she was quickly promoted to be one of the show's booking producers. Reliable, trustworthy, quick, and scrappy, Daniela always got the job done and done right. It didn't matter if the task at hand was big or small. There was a certain type of intensity about her that impressed me.

Her quick thinking on a moment's notice was on display three months into the job on a traveling show to Chicago, when I realized I'd left an entire bag back in New York City. We were going to an event where I needed to be "camera ready," and there I was, barefaced, in desperate need of help. I panicked and called Daniela. Fifteen minutes later she was knocking on my door with a bag full of new makeup products with everything I needed and colors that matched perfectly. She was always so prepared, even though this was her first time helping to coordinate a traveling show in a city she had never been to before.

As she remembers it: "As I hightailed it back to Mika from a nearby shopping center, all I could think was THANK GOD for my stint as a Mary Kay Consultant!"

With so many entry-level young people coming and going from our show, Daniela found a way to make herself stand out for all the right reasons. She took everything about her job seriously and it ultimately worked to her favor: she quickly gained the trust and respect of those around her. She became an indispensable part of the team.

By the time she went on the road with me during the 2016 primary season, I knew her as an exceptional producer. But what I learned about her personal story, during the trip to Chattanooga, made her even more impressive.

Sitting across from each other that morning during our car ride to the private plane, she asked for my opinion on a project she had been thinking about, a platform and community for millennials who came from underrepresented backgrounds that would provide an inside look at coveted jobs by highlighting professionals who had reached the top of their industries.

"I think it would be great to provide learning tools for young people starting their careers who don't have the proximity or access to mentors and work experience—a mix of interviews and resources for millennials so they can feel they're learning from the professionals they could one day see themselves becoming, despite their circumstances," she explained.

Daniela then offered context on the reasoning behind her potential project. Up until that point, I had seen her as my go-to person on the morning show team who could solve whatever came her way. She was so self-aware and engaged in her work that it was almost scary how she anticipated my needs before I knew what they were. A wardrobe problem at 4 a.m.? She would zip through the hallways of 30 Rock and in minutes it was fixed. From show guest logistics problems and dealing with hard-to-handle publicists to early mornings and late nights, traveling and managing a team of interns and assistants, she did it all with a smile on her face and always had a can-do attitude. I always wondered how she could have all that energy so early in the morning!

But I didn't know much about her background: what came next left me speechless.

Originally from South America, Daniela moved to a small rural town in the middle of Ohio at the age of 11. She came from immigrant parents and had humble beginnings. She didn't have many opportunities to learn from professionals around her: there were no real mentors to show her the ropes. She had to learn and assimilate to the language and local culture on her own.

She constantly fought for experiences that seemed out of reach. Not only was she constrained by her socioeconomic background, but geographically, she felt stuck in the middle of a small town, making it hard for her to find exposure to valuable shadowing experience.

Making things more difficult was her legal status...or the lack thereof.

Until she became a DACA recipient, a beneficiary of President Obama's Deferred Action Executive Order allowing undocumented, hardworking young men and women like her to obtain a work permit, she lacked the basic rights and opportunities that many take for granted. Because of the limbo she found herself in through no fault of her own, she couldn't legally work, travel, drive, or ask for loans, and was ineligible for government scholarships to aid her college tuition.

"When I realized the reality of my situation, I had two choices—accept the constant state of restriction I lived in, or be creative about the opportunities I created for myself that didn't necessarily exist. I worked from the bottom up in everything I did."

Against all odds, Daniela managed to go to college, accepting the fact that she would have to be patient, by taking a semester off to work in jobs that paid cash. Even on move-in day at school, she was winging it: "I was the first one from my family to go to an American college. I didn't really get the memo when it came to the nuances of it all and what to expect.

6

"I arrived with a suitcase of clothes and a recycled brown box full of canned goods, organized by a family friend. Meanwhile, my roommates arrived with the type of things that made you feel like you're going to stay awhile: a build-it-yourself shelf for books, a shoe rack, and extra things to make the room homey, like frames for photos, cute flowered pencil holders, an alarm clock, and a rug for those cold wood dorm floors. The majority of my space was claimed by a plastic box with a lock I invested in for my Mary Kay business (this would be one of my lifelines!), a $59.99 buy from Walmart."

Even before she got to school, she didn't know if she could make it for the four years: "I knew it wasn't possible financially; but I didn't think about that, because if I had, I would have come to the realization that there was no possible way for me to go. I did what I always did in a moment of insecurity, distress, confusion—a fear of the 'what ifs': I went into problem-solving, autopilot mode. Instead of wasting time thinking about my legal situation or lack of finances, I started putting everything in place as if it were going to happen—setting myself up to succeed if by chance things did work out."

Without even telling her parents at first, she'd made her way the three hours from Lima, Ohio, to Miami University of Ohio in Oxford, where a program that recruited and hosted high-achieving minority talent on campus had extended an invitation. The three-day engagement promised an automatic $2,500 scholarship for the first year, should she apply and be accepted. It was a glimmer of hope. The money was nothing close to the $20,000 yearly tuition, but it was something.

Although she started without the full funds to finish the school year, she'd saved enough cash from summer and after-school jobs to pay for the first semester. The rest would be a prayer, and efforts to find private scholarships wherever she could.

She forged ahead in a constant state of anxiety, with a knot in her stomach: "Even if I didn't know how it would all play out, I was doing everything in my power, and sometimes more than I thought I was capable of doing, just to make things work—to put myself in a position to have a shot."

Then she encountered a major roadblock while making deliveries for her skin care business as a Mary Kay Consultant and independent contractor. In just one summer, she had saved up a big chunk of what it would cost to start her second year of college as a sophomore at Miami University. Out on deliveries, she hit an unexpectedly steep curve and panicked, pushing on the gas instead of the brake and hitting the fender of the parked car in front of her. In no position to argue with the car's owner, she paid for the damage in cash—the same amount she'd saved all summer to go back to college for her second year.

As she remembers: "I felt numb and helpless. I've never felt so defeated and shaken in my life. I remember being picked up by my mother and parking in an empty Ray's supermarket lot, weeping uncontrollably. My usually unemotional mother broke down with me. Holding each other, we shared an overwhelming sense of helplessness. It was my mom's breakdown that made me suddenly question whether everything would work out. Seeing her break down shook me. She was the anchor and rock in difficult times, the voice that soothed a situation with a 'we'll get through this' mentality.

"I had tried my best, found solutions for myself, and now in one moment it all seemed to disappear. And because of my status, there was no safety net."

Daniela realized she wouldn't be going back to school that fall for her second year—not yet.

That failure would ultimately become a source of strength: "Something powerful happens when you come to the realization that you really are the only person who can change your course—that it really *is* up to you. That you can take charge of your future. That at the end of the day, your willpower comes from within you. I never let the realities in front of me, however restrictive they were, dictate my ability to change them. Your ability to make choices and options is greater than other people's opinions or your own limited environment or baggage."

> Something powerful happens when you come to the realization that you really are the only person who can change your course—that it really *is* up to you. That you can take charge of your future. That at the end of the day, your willpower comes from within you.
>
> —DANIELA PIERRE-BRAVO

She feels that this willpower, inner confidence, and a take-charge mentality are not uncommon in women of her generation, who have a strong desire to make a difference, to find a use for their ambitions and vision for themselves: "Nowadays, young women don't fit into molds or stereotypes. Our courses curve and change, but our ambition and need to make our purpose count will always drive us to succeed if we listen to ourselves closely enough.

"I stopped victimizing myself. I picked myself up and spent the months I would have spent as a sophomore at home working instead. I ramped up my work hours and cold calls to prospective clients for my business. It was a solid 8 a.m. to 10 p.m. workday, six or sometimes seven days a week. But after those five months, not only did I return to school; I was also a changed person with a strong sense of inner confidence. Not the type of confidence that makes you okay with your bad haircut, but the type that makes you resilient in the face of setbacks. This new sense of self brought me clarity. I realized I needed to stop fighting my situation and create another road around my obstacles."

Remarkably, she graduated a semester ahead of schedule. She did so without any loans, government aid, or college tuition debt. Instead, she worked through the summers, sacrificing time off and forgoing vacations. She worked her Mary Kay business throughout school and took part-time side jobs as a bar back in her college town to make ends meet for her tuition and board. She also thought outside the box to help pay for tuition and board. She scoured through private scholarships to apply for, entered creative writing contests for cash prizes, and applied to organizations that supplemented her room and board. Hungry to fight for her education, she made it work. And her road to NBC was just as remarkable; I was astounded by what I was hearing.

The summer before she graduated, she still didn't have any certainty that her legal status would be fixed. For all she knew, the hard work and sacrifice she had made up until that point could have been in vain. Still, she had a plan.

Early on, Daniela had plans to move to a bigger city, knowing it would increase her chances to find valuable shadowing and networking opportunities. She quickly set her sights on New York. Months before her last summer in college, she sent out her résumé to internship programs in media companies and PR and marketing agencies. She understood the importance of having one or two big company names to help validate the rest of her résumé. She also knew that her chances for a first-round interview would be heightened if the hiring managers had the assurance that she was local, making her flexible for interview times. On her résumé she included the address of an NYC college dorm, where she technically expected to live if she ended up receiving a summer internship offer.

Daniela not only got callbacks for interview inquiries, but also ended up on the list of her top two company choices: MTV and Sean "Diddy" Combs's Blue Flame Agency, part of Combs Enterprises. The hiring manager at Combs asked if she could come the next day for an interview. Without thinking twice, Daniela accepted.

"I was so overwhelmed with excitement that I forgot I was still in the middle of Oxford, Ohio, and that I couldn't just jump on a plane and get there in two hours. A few minutes later, I was on the Greyhound bus website booking the next bus out," she explains.

She used the next eighteen hours on the bus to study every angle of the companies, and prep for any potential interview curveballs. She didn't really have the opportunity for a second chance: all her eggs were in one basket. Arriving at New York's Port Authority bus station an hour before her interview, Daniela cleaned herself up and changed in the bus station's public restroom, making sure she was interview-ready.

Surprised and impressed when she confessed her commute from Ohio, the staff at Blue Flame greeted her warmly. All the hours of research and preparation had finally paid off. When she received an email with an official internship offer a few days later, she was elated and eager to start, even if it meant doing the grunt work.

She observes: "I made a lot of coffee runs, as well as organizing and running errands. I was a fish out of fresh water. I remember being asked to go out and get some decorative coffee-table books for one of Mr. Combs's brand activation events. Back then I didn't know what a coffee-table book was! There were lots of 'figure it out' moments during the internship. But it didn't matter, because it was my way *in* the door. It was the experience I needed to stand out, to absorb—to learn how others communicated and how they reacted and acted day-to-day in an office environment."

Daniela's hard work and commitment to her own success proved to be worth it. Not only did she get the internship offer for the summer from Diddy's offices, she also managed to get the other internship at the top of her list, Viacom Media Networks, working for MTV and VH1. In preparation for this summer opportunity, Daniela had saved up for what she knew would be hefty lodging fees to live for a few months in New York City. She did anything she could to make money to support herself for those unpaid internships. She babysat and walked dogs. And when that wasn't enough, she helped promote events at bars and clubs on nights and weekends.

Once she found a smidgen of hope, she clung to it for dear life.

"I remember some days, packing lunch in my purse, and using my internship lunch hours to walk dogs. It was a lot of hard work, but I didn't feel any burden. I was getting my foot in the door and getting valuable exposure I wouldn't have had otherwise. I was grateful just to be there."

Unbelievable!

Sitting at her desk during one of her internships that summer, she remembers getting a text from a family member back in Ohio: "Turn on the TV now."

At that moment President Obama was delivering an official White House statement issuing an executive action of protection for undocumented people like Daniela, which meant they would get a work permit, and could apply for a driver's license and a state ID.

She recalls that she felt numb: "But this time, the numbness turned into euphoria, a type of overwhelming relief, joy, and intense gratitude. Everything from that moment on would be different. I finally had options—real options!—for myself. Everything I had done before then would have the chance to pay off. I finally had the chance to use my degree. Hiding the tears of joy at my desk, I patiently waited until the end of my day to break out in a dance."

Heading back to school that semester, she applied confidently for jobs. Her work permit would arrive right around her graduation—just in time. In the meantime, she applied to the coveted Page Program at NBCUniversal, though she'd heard how tough and competitive it was to get in: "You really don't stand a chance if you don't know anyone that works in the BIZ," read a comment on an online message board.

"The prestigious program is statistically harder to get in to than Harvard University," another article read.

Still, Daniela had a deep desire to work in media, "To be a storyteller, to work creatively and be part of how culture is shared, told, and shaped. But before that summer, I considered it out of reach. But then again, hadn't it felt like everything was out of reach then? I convinced myself to apply."

A phone interview later, she was back on a Greyhound to New York City, this time headed to 30 Rockefeller Center for her final interview for the NBC Page Program. A few weeks later, the program sent her a job offer. With her work permit finally in hand, she accepted.

The rest is history.

After rotating throughout different departments at NBCUniversal including Marketing and Promotions for MSNBC, working in the talent department of *Saturday Night Live*, assisting in audience coordination for *Late Night with Jimmy Fallon*, and other special projects within the company, she ended up at *Morning Joe*.

Daniela's story is not only remarkable because of the sacrifices and guts she showed to achieve her goals, but that she did so while knocking down stereotypical traits inevitably associated with her generation: being entitled, lazy, or self-involved.

And we've got to be honest about this: the stereotypes exist in part because there are young adults who come into the workplace and think they are above getting the coffee. They imagine that they're ready to move up after a month or two on the job. And their workplace demeanor could use work.

But the reality is that most of Daniela's generation isn't like that and doesn't identify with these stereotypes. And they shouldn't feel defined by them.

Approximately 1 in 5 (21 percent) millennial women under 30 say that *entitled* is a word that describes them—while twice that number used words like *underestimated* (41 percent), *driven* (41 percent), *passionate* (47 percent), and *socially conscious* (48 percent) (Harvard Kennedy School IOP, Fall 2017 Survey).

Ultimately, her story impressed me because her background conditioned her from early on to shatter stereotypes. Her unwillingness to accept limits on her goals was a source of confidence. As she puts it: "I never felt defined by being undocumented, not being able to afford the things my friends could, not coming from a well-connected family, or by being a young Latina trying to enter a tough industry without contacts. Stereotypes don't sit well with me because they don't make sense to me. Everyone has a choice on the path they can take, but you have to understand your power in defining your own story."

Everyone has a choice on the path they can take, but you have to understand your power in defining your own story.
—DANIELA PIERRE-BRAVO

Daniela's story is important because it's one many young people might share as they struggle to get access to opportunities, struggle financially, or feel marginalized. Or perhaps they have the connections and networks but don't know how to navigate them. Maybe they're exacerbating stereotypes in subtle ways that need to be corrected; or maybe their roadblocks are psychological. We've all been there—you're not alone.

We're going to help you focus on what you need to do to turn those stereotypes on their head and learn to navigate this crazy (and exciting!) journey in the new world of work.

Working with Daniela, first as a coordinator on the show and now as a collaborator, has shown me the value young working professionals can bring if they come in with the right tools—including their attitude, a sense of professionalism, and a focus on achieving success. You want to come across as someone who can define and execute tasks, solve problems, or provide service efficiently. It will give you leverage to build your career the way Daniela has.

Looking confident and competent comes from showing that

you're listening, being engaged and not distracted, following up promptly, and answering questions completely. It also means, when you're starting out, knowing your role in relation to those around you and using it to support the greater group or the person you report to. Daniela understood all that from the start and leveraged her position to make the team around her more efficient and effective.

Her backstory and her eagerness to succeed inspired me to write this book. She is a great example of the right road map to take as a young professional.

I have given her a space to grow her brand within Know Your Value and share her story in the hopes that other young women will learn from the way she was able to navigate her environment so effectively. Daniela's success is based partly on her profound understanding of how to be self-aware in terms of the abilities and skills she possesses, while at the same time understanding her environment and how to engage and present herself. She debunks the negative stereotypes associated with millennials and instead highlights their assets and strengths.

When she joined our staff, Daniela did so with conviction. She had fought hard to get herself in, so when she was given the chance to produce, she meant business. Her demeanor was professional, serious, and purposeful. And that impressed me.

That's the drive and professional demeanor I encourage young women to have from the get-go in order to stand out. Be focused, and take any tasks in front of you seriously, no matter how menial they seem to you: they mean something to someone. And eventually you'll get to where you want to be; but let your drive, conviction, and eagerness to be there show. Stereotypes should be kicked to the curb from the get go.

Be focused, and take any tasks in front of you seriously, no matter how menial they seem to you: they mean something to someone.

As you try to navigate the road ahead, it's important to build a strong foundation in the workplace like Daniela has, to ensure you can take up the bigger challenges down the road. It all goes back to the central message of what I advocate for women: Know and understand your value. Be able to communicate it. But first, you have to grow it—and *then* figure out what that value is! Because when you do—like Daniela—there is little that can stop you.

As she puts it, her generation has to take the time "to silence our distractions and quiet the naysayers (which sometimes come from inside our own heads) to build up confidence in ourselves.

"When we do that, the only voices we'll hear are our own; that's when we'll know which of our values make us stand out. For me, the values that made me strong in the face of obstacles, that brought me confidence and success, were being resilient and scrappy—a true problem-solver. And once I was able to acknowledge and truly live through those values, I found that doors opened for me, even if I had to start by going through the side door."

CHAPTER TWO

GETTING YOUR FOOT
IN THE DOOR

I got the television bug early on. It feels like I've always known that this was what I wanted to do with my life. But the TV business was, and still is, is a tough one to tap. Getting my foot in the door after college proved incredibly difficult; I really struggled to get my first job. I was shocked to discover that it didn't get any easier, even though I went to the "right" college.

Getting into college wasn't exactly a walk in the park, either.

I am guessing most people would assume that the credentials of my father, who had the honor of serving as National Security Advisor for President Jimmy Carter, would give me my pick of colleges. But I had learning disabilities and struggled in school; I worked really hard just to get by.

Finding a place for myself started with acknowledging that I didn't fit the mold of the rest of my family. I had to embrace my unique talents and skills, and then go out and hone those skills. In the end, I realized that academic achievement isn't the only way to get your foot in the door, and that you can bring other talents to the table.

At first, the pressure from my family was debilitating, because in some ways I felt like such a failure. I always asked myself, "Why?

Why does it seem so much easier for them than it does for me?" Everyone else in the family sailed into college with straight As, while I got rejected from almost every college I applied to. They all went to Ivy League colleges and were Fulbright scholars. My brother Ian, among other things, went on to serve in senior policy positions in the U.S. Department of Defense. My brother Mark is a lawyer and diplomat who was formerly the U.S. ambassador to Sweden. My mother is an artist, a brilliant sculptor. I never felt like I quite measured up to the rest of them.

For the most part, though, having two older brothers and these two incredibly impressive parents was a tremendous blessing. They did not want me to give up, and they did not give up on me.

My mother and grandmother were particularly supportive and encouraged me to try other things. I was a horseback rider, I was a runner, I was in theater, I had jobs in television; I found a way to maximize what I loved and developed my talents outside of school, while also trying to get the best education I could.

I started at Georgetown University, a great college where my father taught (I always wondered if that had something to do with my eventual acceptance…). It was one of the only universities that said yes. But in my heart of hearts, I always knew I wanted to go to Williams College.

I am sure you are thinking, "But Georgetown is an amazing school!" which of course it is and continues to be. My daughter Emilie is currently getting a master's degree in Public Policy there, and I could not be prouder. But to me there was something magical about the Williams campus, with its beautiful open spaces and brick buildings. Being an avid long-distance runner back then, I found myself dreaming of running along those beautiful hills. I wanted to go somewhere that was solely MINE. Something I earned completely on my own merit.

And most important, Williams had given me a big fat "no." I don't respond to "no" well. After getting rejected (twice!), I finally got wait-listed as a transfer student my junior year. But I wasn't satisfied.

Knowing that being wait-listed was probably going to be my last shot at attending, I worked the sidelines and continued to try to get noticed. I had to prove that even though I didn't get perfect grades, I was worth consideration. I continued developing my skills. I was really driven to fill in the blanks on my report card, which had Bs and C+s. I focused on the fact that I was great at theater, and that I had already started my broadcasting résumé doing internships during overnight hours in the summer. I even had my own TV show as a senior in high school.

I needed Williams College to notice how determined, goal-oriented, and serious I was. I had to get to campus and make noise about my application—to let them know how earnestly I wanted to be accepted.

I created my own path, through a side door.

Every year, the Williamstown Theater Festival takes place over the summer on the campus of Williams College in Williamstown, Massachusetts. I decided to take advantage of the proximity to make myself known to the gatekeepers of the college.

Still wait-listed, I worked as an apprentice at the theater festival the summer of my junior year. I was Rob Lowe's apprentice, and I also worked with Christopher Walken and Christopher Reeve. I was thrilled at the chance to do something I knew and loved. At the same time, I was determined to show Williams why I deserved to be taken off the wait list. I wasn't going to wait for anyone to do it for me. They weren't going to get rid of me yet!

To be noticed by the admissions office, I decided to go straight to the top, to the president of the college.

Every day I would go running past the president's house. I literally banged on his door every day. He never responded. But I left a message every day. "Could you tell him Mika Brzezinski is here? I'm on the wait list and I really want to go to Williams!"

I made sure I did everything I could to get their attention, so they knew just how much I wanted to be admitted. The housekeepers noticed my persistence, and eventually they relayed my messages.

"Mika Brzezinski came by," they would tell Williams's president. And then the next day, "Mika Brzezinski came by...again."

Finally, I started to get the attention of people key to the college's admissions department. Word went out that I was at the theater festival. The school started looking into my extracurricular activities and work experience. Soon, it was clear that I had talents that couldn't be measured by just looking at my GPA.

The void that my GPA created on my résumé was filled by a flurry of jobs, talents, and projects.

My scrappiness, my persistence, and the way I kept cultivating my talents wherever I could helped me get my foot in the door— not banging my head against the wall trying to be a perfect student. That was never going to happen for me.

After a hot, sweaty summer at the Williamstown Theater Festival, I drove back to D.C. to return to Georgetown.

A day before my junior year started, I got pulled off the wait list at Williams College! I was ecstatic. Before I knew it, I was back in Williamstown, this time to start the fall semester. I just got in my Nissan Stanza and headed up the highway to MY new school!

But it didn't get easier. During my time at Williams, I'll admit that I didn't get the greatest grades. In fact, I barely graduated. I was so grateful to be there, as hard as the courses were. I wanted to surround myself with excellence and try to measure up—even if I didn't, most of the time. The experience taught me the importance of working hard and being relentless in the pursuit of the things you want. It showed me how to persevere, no matter how many "nos" you hear in the process.

When I came back to the campus in 2009 to be honored with the Bicentennial Medal, an award given to alumni with distinguished achievements in their field, I was so touched; this honor meant so much to me.

Engaging with the students on campus that day, I saw myself in many of them at their age: eager, hopeful, and probably a bit apprehensive about their futures. It was a great day meeting them and telling them this story. I felt so thankful to be honored for something I had fought so hard for, long ago.

My college experience taught me to be persistent in finding a way forward, even if you don't see one at first. It taught me to be tough, and to fight for the opportunities I wanted—a type of resilience that proved to be so important in setting the tone for my career. And you may have to find ways to get yourself through several doors as you navigate the workplace. I sure did! While

I don't necessarily recommend stalking people at their homes, showing people that you care, and that you are not giving up, is crucial. That's why building resilience and being okay with rejection is actually beneficial to moving forward in your career.

My coauthor, Daniela, had so many obstacles in her path. Neither she nor anyone in her family had the finances or capability to apply for financial aid. But instead, she was scrappy in finding ways to make it work. No loans? She found odd jobs to pay for college in cash and got any and every scholarship she could. She had to dig deep: $500 for a creative writing entry, a leadership scholarship to finance her lodging, and independent research. You name it; she did it. These small scholarships paid off in a big way.

Even more difficult, she was the first person in her family to graduate from an American college. She didn't have anyone to show her the ropes or help with applications or financing options. Daniela constantly researched ways to help herself, and always had a plan B and a plan C if things didn't work out the first time.

She didn't have a safety net or a guide to get her in the door anywhere. Early on, she learned to see obstacles as opportunities. That's the spirit of winners, and that's why she's excelled at every single task I gave her, from the beginning of our work together to the execution of this book. The message to your generation is this: it's always about finding a side door if you can't get your foot in the front.

The first year I tried to get a job in TV, I practically lived out of my car. I applied to every TV station I could with the on-air tapes from a cable access show I put on in

Fairfax County, Virginia, when I was a senior in high school. I also used tapes from my short stint at Williams, when I did a cable access show in North Adams, Massachusetts, on teen pregnancy. Because my grades hadn't been the greatest, I wanted my résumé and my activities outside of school to show that I was engaged and focused on my career. I got a great education and an English degree, and built a very strong TV résumé before I even graduated from college.

...it's always about finding a side door if you can't get your foot in the front.

Even so, I still couldn't get a job.

I drove all over the country with those tapes. Everybody told me they weren't good enough. I even went to Presque Isle, Maine, the smallest market in the country. They wouldn't hire me! I needed "more experience."

After a year of looking for a television job that way, and traveling to remote towns, I took a $100 gig at Vermont ETV for a month in Burlington, Vermont. To support myself, I had side gigs in the offices of then Governor Madeleine Kunin and her press secretary. I was determined to make it work, even if it wasn't exactly what I wanted to do.

Here is the lesson I learned when you don't have a network or don't know where to start: you fill in a blank where you can, and gradually get to where you need to go. And by the way—you don't have to figure it out right at the beginning! That's just a way to create stress before you even get going.

Facing Challenges

In that memorable conversation with Daniela on the car ride to the private plane, she caught my attention by advocating for women who lack access to people who could help them break into the careers they want. That motivated us to take a second look at the barriers that hold young women back—not everybody can just knock on a door or send an email and expect a response.

> Our polling in collaboration with Harvard Kennedy School's Institute of Politics (Fall 2017) shows the sense of anxiety over getting your foot in the door. Women with degrees from public colleges and universities feel more prepared to perform well (43 percent) compared to those with degrees from private colleges (33 percent). The research found that only about one in four millennial women between 20 and 29 years old (26 percent) feel prepared for finding their first professional job after graduation.

Ironically, sometimes the women who are best prepared academically have the hardest time breaking into their chosen field.

Women studying STEM (Science, Technology, Engineering, and Mathematics) and entering related fields face some of the hardest challenges for advancement. In the hard sciences in particular, where the leadership ranks are still dominated by men, the entry barriers facing women are many and the climb to the top is especially steep.

In May 2018, The Ohio State University published research showing how young women with higher GPAs, especially in STEM fields, were more likely to be hired if they appeared more likeable, and displayed qualities such as being social or outgoing; whereas their male counterparts were valued most for competence and commitment.

Stellar grades in college can actually hurt women new to the job market in STEM. The study found "Male applicants with high grade point averages were twice as likely to be contacted by employers as women with the same grades and comparable experience and educational background. The picture was even worse for women who majored in math. Male math majors who excelled in school were called back by employers three times as often as their women counterparts."

Employers were skeptical about high-achieving women's personalities. Women with "just good enough" grades but likable personalities did better: "A survey of 261 hiring managers found that while employers value competence and commitment among men applicants, they are prone to gravitate toward women applicants who are perceived as likable—those who did fine, but did not excel, academically. This helps women who are moderate achievers and are often described as sociable and outgoing, but hurts high-achieving women, who are met with more skepticism."

The discouraging conclusion: "While women make up half of the college-educated workforce in the U.S., according to the latest Science & Engineering Indicators from the National Science Foundation, they only comprise 29 percent of those in science and engineering occupations. Modest gains have been made over the past few decades, but the gender gap isn't closing fast enough."

We spoke to Laura Sherbin, managing director at Diversity Best Practices, who has been doing research on the constraints of women in STEM since 2006. She studied to become a chemical engineer but "very quickly realized in my college that it was likely not going to be an industry in which I would have a successful career."

Ultimately, she switched focus and earned a PhD in Economics. She thrived in the field but found it very unsettling that she was deterred from it in the first place: "I didn't believe the industry would love me back," she says. Laura's experience isn't uncommon.

These women have phenomenal academic accolades and are exceedingly smart. They work so hard, and face incredibly difficult challenges due to what Laura describes as an "intrinsic belief that's held by their colleagues, by their leaders, and honestly sometimes held by them themselves, that women are less capable in these fields."

One of the most notorious examples was a 2005 address made by Lawrence Summers, then president of Harvard University, stating that men outperform women in science and math because of genetic differences. Several prominent women scientists walked out of the room.

Some things haven't changed, at least not enough: data show us how prevalent the challenges are for young women today.

Clearly there is pervasive bias, as Laura Sherbin notes: "We heard Larry Summers say it at a Harvard commencement speech. You hear people say it time and time again. It came through pretty loud and clear in the James Damore Google memo," she says, referring to the Google engineer who argued that men are better suited to working in technology than women.

She observes: "This belief that women just aren't cut out to do the work is something that so zaps your confidence every moment of every day, and it almost discounts every value that you bring."

For women who are so driven in their work and so determined to make an impact on their world, "It creates even more of a firestorm and frustration because it inhibits them from doing one thing that they are desperate to do—which is good work—to deliver value to the world," Laura observes.

Women entering the field of law face similar challenges. According to a survey from the American Bar Association conducted by the Center for WorkLife Law at the University of California, Hastings College of the Law, many women and people of color felt they were held to a higher standard than white men.

When it came to equal access to the kind of "high-quality" assignments that lead to exposure and advancement in an organization, 81 percent of white men felt they had access to those opportunities, while only 63 percent of white women felt that way. That percentage dropped even farther for women of color: only 53 percent reported having access to those opportunities.

The women surveyed, independent of their ethnicity, felt they had to keep up a close watch on their behavior to prevent backlash. They experienced pressure to act "in feminine ways" instead of exhibiting stereotypically male behaviors. Consistent with how women are treated industry-wide, these women felt more likely to be given "office housework," like ordering lunch or comforting a colleague in distress.

According to the same research, "women lawyers of color were eight times more likely than white men to report that they had been mistaken for janitorial staff, administrative staff, or court personnel."

The American Bar Association Commission on Women in the Profession reported in 2018 that women accounted for only 35 percent of active American lawyers in 2016. Of the top lawyers for Fortune 500 companies, only 26 percent were women. The same study also found that white women graduate from law school in large numbers, yet only 32 percent account for law school deans.

We all expect and deserve to be treated equally with men, but do we truly believe parity is possible?

> Research we conducted with Harvard pollster John Della Volpe shows that young women are more likely to believe that their job will be replaced by artificial intelligence or a robot in ten years, than that men and women will be treated equally in the workplace (Harvard Kennedy School IOP, Fall 2017 Survey).

That statistic is just plain scary. But young women should know that there has never been a time when they hold more power to undo that thinking.

Eva Longoria, actress, director, producer, and entrepreneur, is also an activist in the Latino community. Through her work with the Eva Longoria Foundation, she has uncovered, through both research and firsthand experience, some of the obstacles that women of color face as they get their start in business. The barriers that continue to hold Latinas back are typically socioeconomic in nature; access to education remains the single most important determinant of Latinas' earning potential, and the intervention that can break the cycle of poverty. Eva shared that 25 percent of Latinas in the U.S. live below the poverty line, and more than 50 percent are classified as very low income. A majority of the young women Eva has worked with first heard the word "college" in high school, when "it is too late to start preparing. They're very late to the game."

Latino communities lack early education centers: "We don't have a lot of preschool education prior to entering elementary in low-income neighborhoods. There are fewer resources and a lot of educational barriers," she adds. These translate to a lack of economic mobility.

Parental engagement is also key. Eva's foundation commissioned a study that found that an important predictor of Latina educational success is having a strong personal belief—supported by your parents—that you will complete high school and attend college: "Having a parent engaged in your educational journey is associated with success."

Latino parents often face additional barriers to getting involved in their children's education in an effective way—whether due to language barriers, long work hours, financial constraints, or lack of familiarity with the local school system. First-generation college students often navigate high school and then college applications with parents who are new to the process themselves.

Research from Harvard's Institute of Politics confirms that among young women entering the workplace, members of the Latino community are far less likely than others to have been raised by parents who have a college degree.

"Honors or AP classes are important on a college application. But not all parents understand this. If a (Latino) student is making straight As in regular courses, their parents look at the report card and say, you're doing great! But it might be on a lower track than would truly challenge the student, so that's unfortunate. Very often (Latino) students must become their own advocates to be placed in honors classes," Eva notes.

The foundation's study also showed that involvement in extracurricular activities helps Latinas develop a sense of belonging at school, where they can frequently feel like outsiders. Participation in extracurricular activities—where they are often in contact with high-performing peers with college-going aspirations—is also associated with higher graduation and college attendance rates for Latina students. Daniela's parents worked two and three jobs and came home exhausted. Every step of the way, she had to advocate for herself.

But women at the other end of the economic spectrum often struggle to gain a foothold in their careers for opposite reasons: many college-educated young women suffer from *too much* parental involvement, leaving them with connections, but not necessarily the know-how to navigate their network on their own or advocate for themselves effectively. Few enter the workplace with any experience in an office, for example; and they may lack work experience entirely. I have encountered plenty of well-connected kids with so-called helicopter parents who are constantly trying to help them, monitor them, push them in all different directions. Most of these young people do well; but others fall behind because they've never had to figure things out for themselves. They haven't learned self-awareness or the proper level of professionalism.

Then there are young women from all walks of life who fail to make the right impression because they bring the way they move in their personal life into the workplace.

The story I told at the start of this book about my former assistant Emily is instructive.

Emily has a large network of friends, an extremely supportive family, and a sunny disposition. Her parents have showered her with support and have made sure she was at ease her whole life. She is used to being liked. She felt entitled to walk into a room and expect the same warmth and openness that she receives in her personal life. But the truth is, in the workplace, people are not going to automatically like you. They may be obligated to show you basic respect and professional cooperation, but they don't have to like you. Assuming that you will walk into a room where everyone inside is waiting to befriend you is the wrong way to approach work relationships.

Ultimately, once Emily learned that being good at her job did not require warmth from her colleagues, her career took off—when the need to be liked stopped holding her back. It made her stronger at work. It allowed her to instead focus on the skills she could use to develop her career. And she found ways to navigate her environment at the start that allowed her to flourish—while still being kind and warm to others.

Just as you have to work your way up into a position, you also have to understand that you need to earn people's perception of you. In truth, you need to walk in the door like you don't know what's around the corner. I'm not saying you should feel scared—rather, that you need to be professional.

The way young women see themselves is key to developing a professional persona that can help them get started. Self-doubt doesn't discriminate—it affects young women from all backgrounds. But one thing is constant: ultimately, you have the power to change your course and take the reins of your career. But at the very start of your career, when your network is limited, you might have to go out and find a way to build one for yourself.

Building Connections and Networking Effectively

The good news is that just as there is no linear path to a successful career, there is no one way to get your foot in the door. At least in the age of social media, you can meet and connect with professionals online to find ways into the industries you want, and initiate relationships with professionals who can help you get there.

We all know connections can make a huge difference in your career, but breaking the professional ice with strangers can be intimidating.

> Our research with Harvard showed that only about a third (35 percent) of millennial women between 20 and 29 feel confident networking.

Vanessa De Luca, former editor in chief of *Essence* magazine, advises young millennials to start by targeting a group rather than an individual: "There are so many organizations right now that are all about connecting like-minded women within an industry." She shares examples like ColorComm, Her Agenda, and the bSmart Guide. "Reach out to one of those organizations and get involved in some way; either become a member or attend some of their meetings and meet some people."

Your ultimate goal is to connect with people who will vouch for you and introduce you to other people who might open up career opportunities eventually: "Just being in a room with people trying to do the same thing, and then being vocal about what I'm interested in, has always worked for me," says Vanessa.

Executive coach Liz Bentley shared a few examples of people who got in the door of big companies by doing just that: "One of my clients landed a job at at a prestigious company with no connections—and did it through LinkedIn. There were two or three companies she wanted to get into, so she created alerts to give her information on news and personnel updates in the specific departments within companies she was pursuing. She especially focused on one of the rising leaders and eventually got an interview with him. He was so impressed with her knowledge of him, his team, and the organization, that she got the job. Since then she has been promoted numerous times. If you don't have a connection, you just have to work a little harder and be more creative."

Reaching Out

Daniela shares that when she was trying to build a professional network, it was harder because she didn't have the resources to connect with professional women. She would send "cold" emails and get on buses to travel to New York City and take informationals when she could, and place phone calls to people willing to speak to her about their industries.

Now that she's in management herself, Daniela has supervised the hiring of interns on *Morning Joe*. Recent graduates hoping to get jobs in the media industry connect with her by adding her on LinkedIn, and then use their InMail service to reach out. She says, "There are emails and messages I'll receive that make it easy for me to engage, and others that make it tougher for me to reply. It's all in the tone.

"The biggest mistake you can make is reaching out to someone in a big company without expressing any sort of connection or purposefulness. If your goal is to get an internship, for instance, at the very least you should do some research on the department in which you'd like to work."

I couldn't agree with her more. When you're reaching out to someone, make your communication focused, clear, and substantive. After all, the person at the other end is taking time out of his or her day to read your email, and in the best-case scenario, agreeing to meet you or make an introduction. Make it worth his or her time.

Daniela shared two cold emails she received on LinkedIn from young women to demonstrate this point.

Hi Daniela,

I am wondering if you have any advice or connections in helping me obtain a position with NBCUniversal or if you can help point me in the right direction to do so?

"This email is very hard for me to answer. First, if she'd done her research, she would have known that NBCUniversal has many different divisions and departments. There is no way for me to point her in the right direction if she doesn't refer to a specific job opening or even mention an area of the company. Is she interested in a specific show? A business division? I can't tell by this correspondence. Second, there is no personal connection to this email. The tone is very 'what can you do for me?' I would assume that this was copied and pasted to a number of different people."

Unless you're reaching out to a member of the Human Resources department, the recipient of a cold email has no particular motivation to learn about you. Help your potential contacts help you by giving them a reason to read through your résumé—make that link, and your purpose, clear.

That's not to say you can't start networking if you don't know exactly where you may want to end up. You should certainly try to connect online with companies and people who interest you, especially if you are still trying to figure out what career path to take. But as always, it's important to be gracious and respectful of their time and how you ask for it.

Here is another example of a message Daniela received that not only resulted in a response, but after an informational meeting and a few coffee dates, she personally recommended this young woman to the NBC Page Program. Now the young woman that once cold-messaged Daniela on LinkedIn works as a producer on the *Today* show. Her name has been changed to respect her privacy.

Hi Daniela,

My name is Jennifer Hastings and I just graduated from Miami University in May. I have been exploring career opportunities at NBCUniversal and came across your profile on LinkedIn as we have a few mutual connections from Miami! I am currently interning at a public relations agency in NYC but am looking for opportunities this September. I would love the chance to talk to you about your time at NBC or just to reminisce about Miami! Please let me know if you would be interested in grabbing coffee or chatting on the phone and I look forward to hearing from you soon.

All the best,
Jennifer

How was this young woman so effective in her communication? "Her email felt personalized and genuine," Daniela says.

"She made the connection that we both went to the same university and had mutual contacts. And the fact that she mentioned that she was looking for opportunities is not a bad thing; we were all there once. The difference is how and why she asked for my time. She asked to hear about my own experience at the company instead of jumping to conclusions that I would automatically recommend her for jobs. There was less pressure.

"More people are willing to give you their time if you ask to learn about their background in a genuine way."

SVP and Chief People Officer Christina Hall, head of the Global Talent Organization at LinkedIn, oversees the hiring and development of top talent. She offers this about how individuals she doesn't know have successfully gotten a response from her: "Rather than just sending a request (through LinkedIn) without context, send an invite with a message there explaining why they're interested in connecting with me. It doesn't always have to be about their experience or their career."

Following and connecting with HR professionals through social media can also be used as a resource even if you are not looking for a job from them. Daniela shares this advice: "If you're trying to get a sense of a work culture or a leg up on how to talk to professionals in the industries they work in, whether they're recruiters or HR professionals, try following them on sites like Twitter or connect on LinkedIn. They often share articles and pieces on industry trends, interview tips, highlight important people from their companies, as well as overall resources that will give you the industry know-how. This all might come in handy when you're thinking about talking points when connecting with people in that industry. It might also give you leads on who to connect with internally, or you might find a job opening on their latest post or feed."

There are other proactive steps you can take to build relationships with LinkedIn members. After following the person on the platform, Hall recommends staying engaged: "Provide commentary to anything I post on there. I tend to post articles about things I'm doing at work or share something pertinent to an issue I'm addressing with the leader of our global talent organization here. If I see someone adding a great thought about it or expanding upon a topic that makes me interested, it often allows for a dialogue with someone I haven't met before."

Cindi Leive, former editor in chief of *Glamour* and *Self* magazines, acknowledges that reaching out to someone for the first time isn't easy: "It's always, by definition, a little awkward."

Cindi suggests asking yourself these questions: "Are you asking for advice? Are you asking for a connection to somebody? Are you asking to be considered for a position that's open? It's important to know what you're going for, and to be clear about that."

Another thing to think about: do you really need an in-person meeting, or will an email exchange be helpful? "If it's somebody that you really don't know, but they're in your business, and they've expressed that they want to be connected, that's great. But they don't have time for coffee with someone they don't know. They may not even have time for a personal conversation, so think about whether that really is necessary."

And if you want your work to be noticed by someone you don't know? Cindi gives this effective example: "If you're an aspiring producer and you have a documentary project that you work on in your spare time, you might choose to send a clip of that or coverage of that to somebody in that field who has a specific interest in your subject area."

Then add why this person might be interested in looking at this specific project or proposal you're working on. You have to do some homework before you can make the bridge, to establish the purpose of connecting.

Being clear in your message, and why it makes sense for the person you are contacting to look over your work, is essential. Be clear about what you are asking, and why. And it shouldn't look like you've sent the same file or request to hundreds of different people.

Cindi says, "Even if you just want to connect by saying, 'I just want to tell you how much I admire you and thanks for inspiring me' or 'I'm looking for a job in this field, I'd love to keep in touch with you,' that's fine too. Just make it personal."

We asked a recruiter at BuzzFeed, one of the most coveted millennial-centric media companies, for a few ways to create a meaningful connection with a potential job lead.

First and foremost, the recruiter stressed, be appreciative of your potential contact's time. Don't assume that they can meet with you in person—offer them the option of a phone call, or if you are making a connection in person, ask if you can follow up via email. Make your request easy for them and be flexible.

The BuzzFeed recruiter also offers this tip: Find a person who works in the job that interests you, rather than emailing a recruiter. "Yes, the recruiter's job is to hire people...but if someone is looking to understand the life experience that led to a particular position, I'd encourage the job seeker to find a contact who's already doing what they're looking to do, and reach out directly in a very intentional way."

Just as Daniela responded positively to a young woman who made a personal connection and approached with respect and courtesy, you'll get the best results by being as specific as possible in your request. Not every one-off phone call or meeting will turn into a job offer or even a job referral, of course—but you never know.

Informationals

Informational meetings can be a great way to get real traction in your job search. You have the opportunity to get in front of someone who works at the company where you want to work, even if there isn't necessarily a job opening. The lack of a job opening is both a bad thing and a good thing. It's a good thing because you have nothing to lose—so go ahead and ask the questions that will help you present yourself in the best light when the job finally becomes available.

As an executive coach, Liz Bentley gets plenty of questions on the right approach to making the most out of informational meetings. "Make those meetings very action-oriented, with two specific goals: 1. Grow yourself by learning about the company, the industry, and the career track of the person with whom you are meeting. 2. Make a good impression so that they will pass you along for another informational meeting or job opportunity. If you're not getting traction, you have to create traction."

If you're not getting traction, you have to create traction.
—LIZ BENTLEY

Liz's advice: "The key is to be a great listener but also a great conversationalist. Before the meeting, do your homework and create a bank of questions. Study the person, know the company, know the basics of the job. Ask yourself, 'What am I trying to learn from this specific candidate?'"

Liz Bentley highlights two approaches to creating good questions in informational interviews: questions that address the tactical side of the business and job, and the personal side of the person's experience in their career.

Tactical: These are questions that speak to the skill set of the job; what it takes to do the job, what makes the job interesting, and how the job works.

For example, if someone is in banking, mergers and acquisitions, you might be asking about what they do, how they do it, and the types of clients they work with. This covers all the technical pieces of doing the job well and the qualities they look for when hiring. Which candidates stand out and why?

If someone's in media, say, as a writer, a few tactical questions might focus on the kind of articles they write. How might the entry-level staffers work their way up to writing features? What are the steps to becoming a successful writer in the industry?

If you are speaking to someone in a higher-level position and are sitting down in an informational, try asking about their own career evolution: What was their career journey? How did they weave it all together? Which skill sets took them from one level to another? Are the skills that made them successful still key today, or do entry-level workers have to bring something more or different to succeed? What if anything were the surprises that helped them succeed?

You might also ask a few big-picture questions along the lines of: "Where do you see this industry trending? Where has it been historically, and where do you see it going?"

Liz points out: "I think it's important to recognize that every single industry is completely changing. Fifty percent of jobs today won't be here in the near future. There's no industry that's immune; they are all being significantly impacted. Having them talk about their vision of where their industry and company are going will often set you apart. Leaders are talking about this all the time; so not only will you look smart, but you will also learn a lot about future trends that can help you on your career track and in future interviews."

These tactical questions can give you a better sense not only of the starting position, but how you could progress into a higher one. Liz suggests taking advantage of this moment, when no job is at stake, to find out "what the first levels of the business look like, and how people evolve in those spaces."

Asking broader questions—even about pay—in informational interviews can help you envision a career track that you haven't previously considered.

When Liz was looking for an entry-level role, she was deciding between sales and marketing, and decided to ask about salaries in her informational meetings. As it turned out, "the sales salary was double or triple the marketing salary 5–10 years into the job. That was really helpful because everyone was pushing women into marketing and men into sales.

"If I hadn't asked that question, I never would have known. No one had ever explained to me that the closer you are to making money for the company, the more you're going to be paid. So asking that question was pivotal to understanding the long-term decision I was making and the tactics of how this is going to work."

Personal: These questions are all about making you stand out. "If you ask smart, tactical questions, you look competent and capable. But if you ask personal questions, you will learn what makes people tick," Liz says. She isn't suggesting you ask people intrusive questions about their personal lives, but rather, ask questions that prompt them to talk about the emotions they ascribe to their jobs—this approach tends to get people talking about themselves, which helps foster a connection.

Liz suggests you throw in some less invasive questions to start and gauge how the person feels about answering them before moving on to questions like, "What is it that inspires you? Which qualities made you successful? Who were your mentors?"

A few other examples:

"What is it that you love about doing this business and/or the work? What point in your career made you realize that this is what you were meant to do?"

"What makes this career frustrating or difficult? What challenges have you overcome to continue to thrive in it? What are some of the barriers you've had to face?"

All of these questions "get people really talking and thinking about things in a way they haven't in the past. I think they are used to the tactical questions and assume everyone's going to ask them," Liz says.

If you have an established relationship with someone who is offering you professional advice, make sure you also go in prepared. Carla Harris, vice chairman and managing director at Morgan Stanley and author of *Strategize to Win: The New Way to Start Out, Step Up, or Start Over in Your Career*, advises millennials who go into advisory meetings with senior people to "go in with an agenda. Senior people will value the fact that you have specific questions you'd like to discuss. I'm very up-front and transparent about that.

"A meeting with me often ends up being a very productive conversation, because they say, 'I've heard I need to have an agenda. I wrote down my five questions.'

"Sometimes they have twelve. They walk away satisfied, because they engaged with me, and got to know me a little bit. I'm very happy because I feel fulfilled; they got what they were looking for when they came in. Without fail, I say, 'Hey, I like where you're going. Why don't we get together in six to eight weeks?' Or 'Keep me posted, drop me an email.'"

Whether you are going in for an exploratory interview or just asking for advice from someone who might help open a door in your career, they are both an opportunity to learn and grow while the pressure's off. They're great practice and can often lead to bigger things.

CHAPTER THREE

NAILING THE INTERVIEW

You've made that key first contact for an entry-level job or a key internship, and you've gotten your chance to apply: now comes the formal interview. It's time to knock it out of the park and make the right impression. Everything matters: from the clothes you select to the way you step in the door to your body language and demeanor.

You've got to own it. Every part of your presentation.

Yes, it's nerve-racking; but few have had to go through what Daniela did to get started. Groggy after taking four buses through the night, she arrived in bustling Times Square in the heart of New York City from Ohio. Taking her carefully chosen interview clothes, she cleaned up and changed in the bathroom at the Port Authority bus terminal.

This, she thought, would be her last chance to gain an internship before graduating from college.

Living in the Midwest for so long, and never having worked in New York City, Daniela didn't want to jump to conclusions about how to dress for an interview in music mogul Sean Combs's Bad Boy Entertainment offices. The company, Combs Enterprises, includes a clothing line, a record label, and a marketing agency.

She recalls: "I wasn't quite sure if the environment was casual, business casual, or creative. I picked up through research that because the department where I was interviewing was a marketing division, it must be a combination of all three—which made my understanding of the dress code more confusing. I decided to keep things simple and wore a black pencil skirt, flats, and a neutral-colored top."

Playing it safe, and not bringing too much attention to her clothes and personal style, was one of the best things Daniela could have done. It worked in her favor. All the attention was on what she had to say, not what she was wearing.

When you get farther in your career and are eventually in your second or third job interview, personal style can even set you apart and add to your professional brand. But when you are seeking an internship or entry-level role? KEEP IT SIMPLE!

Style expert and former *Vogue* creative director André Leon Talley has a keen eye for what makes an effective personal presentation, from what you wear to how you present yourself. Often found sitting front-row at major fashion shows, he's influenced designers and artists like Tom Ford and Vivienne Westwood. André agrees that you shouldn't bring too much attention to your clothes when you're just starting out.

And the great thing about it? You don't have to spend a ton for professional work wear: "You can put on a blouse from H&M, or a white shirt from H&M and a simple skirt, or a simple pair of pants from Uniqlo, and just a pair of black shoes."

You want to make sure that your outfit doesn't detract from *you*. And if you're going into an interview in an unfamiliar environment, and you don't have a network inside the company to ask what's appropriate, you don't want to start guessing. You don't want your attire to be distracting for you or the interviewer. So keep it simple, and focus more on preparing for the actual interview, rather than on what you're wearing.

For my book *Grow Your Value,* André gave me an example of an interview misstep that's worth mentioning again.

One young woman, he recalls, came in with head-to-toe designer wear: "The Calvin Klein with the Gucci bracelets, and the right shoe." But instead of being impressed, André noted that: "She spent more time preparing the right brand, or what she thinks I would like, because it's *Vogue,* than the substance when I am asking her questions!"

André says, "You don't have to be dressed in a certain way or dressed to the nines, but you've got to be neat, you've got to be presentable and well-mannered. You've got to have a kind of deportment."

He's seen young professionals who looked like they've "jumped out of bed, put on a wrinkled dress, wore the wrong shoes, tacky jewelry, and mismatched nail polish." It looks sloppy and unprofessional and makes a bad impression.

Above all, your clothing should be comfortable. You should be able to move around and not have to fuss with a top or a skirt mid-interview because the article of clothing feels too tight or doesn't cover the right places. Being uncomfortable in your clothes shows through your body language. It makes you self-conscious and throws off your ability to project confidence.

You don't have to be dressed in a certain way or dressed to the nines, but you've got to be neat, you've got to be presentable and well-mannered. You've got to have a kind of deportment.
—ANDRÉ LEON TALLEY

When it comes to accessories, make sure they're not distracting. Keep accessories subtle and minimal. The first interview isn't the right place for big hoop earrings or dangly bracelets that make noise with every move you make. Again, steer clear of anything that can be seen as distracting.

One accessory forbidden on interviews in André's book? Nose rings. "If you have someone that you're interviewing for an internship and they've got a nose ring? Uh, no thank you, we'll be in touch!"

Presentation and style are only partly about the clothes, as André explained it to me. Making a good impression is dependent on the way you present yourself, the way you carry yourself, and how you interact with the world.

Politeness can go a long way. For example, if you're in an interview and you're checking in with an assistant at the front desk, always be extra courteous to him or her.

"I know of hiring managers who ask their support staff how they were greeted by the job candidates," Daniela adds. Office staffers talk to each other—you have to assume that anyone you meet in a new office may be asked for their impression of you.

And let's not forget body language.

In an interview, when your nerves get the best of you, it's harder to appear calm and collected. Your body automatically goes into defense mode; you are not at ease, and you become stiff. Adjusting your posture and body language helps to convey self-confidence and ease.

But what if you are naturally shy, and get nervous speaking? All you want to do in a group of people is to make yourself invisible. Instead of hunching over, make yourself taller. Work on your posture constantly. On purpose. Force yourself to sit up straight. Stand up tall by tucking in your stomach and imagine that your head is being pulled up by a thread. Shift your shoulders back. It's not going to be comfortable the first few times. It took me years to get the amazing posture I have on television. But I work on it every day.

Why is posture so important? Because it gives you power. Good posture literally strengthens your words. It makes them richer, more robust. Try sitting up straight and delivering a message, and you'll know what I mean. You'll look in control just using and being aware of your body language.

Katty Kay, coauthor with Claire Shipman of *The Confidence Code: The Science and Art of Self-Assurance—What Women Should Know*, is also a presenter on *BBC World News* on PBS. She backs me up on the importance of posture and stance when it comes to exuding power and self-assurance: "Nod, smile, engage; don't mumble, look at the floor, or shuffle around the place."

In fact, if you do these simple moves on a regular basis, Katty says, they build on themselves and improve your confidence long-term. But in the short term, for getting through that half-hour interview, "you just have to force yourself to remember to present yourself in a way that looks, sounds, and feels confident," even if your body is naturally inclined to project feelings of uneasiness or nervousness that make it harder to feel and look self-assured—or worse, hamper your ability to get your message across.

Nail Your Pitch

When you are pitching yourself in an interview, you want to communicate clearly the qualities that make you good for the job and what you would bring to the table.

Daniela explains how she prepared for job interviews early on. "I always had four or five examples of my top strengths and came up with an anecdote or example for each of them. I always made sure I had a quick bio practiced, in case I had to pitch myself on the fly."

Try following this format Daniela used in her own interviews to help guide your pitch: "I'm originally from Lima, Ohio, and went to school to study International Studies because I wanted to learn more about geopolitics and world cultures. Then I realized I had an interest in influencing which stories shape a culture. Given the influence of media, I did an internship at MTV Networks in their ad sales department to get experience in the media industry and learn more about how the business is run.

"I'm the kind of person who always wants to learn how things function from the bottom up. Recently I did a project for a few MTV executives on millennial culture in order to focus on how millennials consume media, and my current goal is to work in content creation to explore that further."

Communicating who you are and what you bring to the table

is even more critical. Practicing a description of what you bring to the table is so important. Say it out loud. Seriously, take out your phone, put it in selfie mode or use a mirror, and start talking about yourself. See how you look while you practice a pitch. And watch how you do it, and how many times you delete it because you're horrified at how you look doing it. Now imagine yourself in a room with someone, talking about yourself: How are you going to do that well if you can't do it alone with your phone?

Find opportunities to practice presenting yourself. Make a toast, or give a speech at a dinner party or wedding. Get comfortable with your voice. Feel the physicality behind it. You won't be good at it at first, but you will be able to visualize and feel what it actually needs to look and feel like when it's "go" time. Practice it, don't wing it.

Find opportunities to practice presenting yourself. Make a toast, or give a speech at a dinner party or wedding. Get comfortable with your voice. Feel the physicality behind it.

Not only will practice help you find the right words to describe all the great things you have to offer, but it will also help you feel more confident next time you need to advocate for yourself in a nerve-racking situation, like an interview or a presentation. Your body will remember, even if your mind is jittery. Being able to deliver a strong and clear message about who you are, and what your value is, makes all the difference.

Understand Your Audience

When you are comfortable in your skin and can articulate your ideas clearly, you should also be able to read your audience. Being in the moment, listening to what's being said and responding thoughtfully, shows you have emotional intelligence. That you understand the complexities of the person you're talking to— and know exactly what they're looking for from you. You put your best foot forward by communicating why you are the best person for the job and how you fit into the equation.

This will come up again and again, whether it's navigating a new environment, delivering an effective presentation, or negotiating at work. You must know and be able to read your audience. Are they nodding, and encouraging you to continue? Are they looking like they're trying to get a word in edgewise? Do they look impatient, as if they want to switch the subject? If you've prepared in advance, you can remain calm enough in an interview to see the signals the interviewer is giving you, and pivot when the interviewer seems to want something more or different.

Being able to engage your audience is a life skill that will stay with you and make you an effective communicator in any situation.

What value am I offering to this job or organization? How useful am I? What are the things I could be doing that make me indispensable? What skills can I develop in this job to become even more valuable down the road?

—CAL NEWPORT

Cal Newport, associate professor at Georgetown University and author of *Deep Work: Rules for Focused Success in a Distracted World* and *So Good They Can't Ignore You: Why Skills Trump Passion in the Quest for Work You Love,* asks young people to think outside their personal concerns in interviews in a way that shows self-awareness. As you go through the interview, try to think about the following: What value am I offering to this job or organization? How useful am I? What are the things I could be doing that make me indispensable? What skills can I develop in this job to become even more valuable down the road?

Keeping in mind these two questions in particular can help you keep your conversation on track: "How can I benefit X organization? What can I learn here that will better my skills?" Use them as a framework to underscore your compatibility with the job, while also exploring the needs of your potential employer.

Demonstrating self-awareness is a strength that opened doors for Daniela early in her career: "When I was interviewing for internships and my first jobs, I always ended with 'Is there anything that you didn't find in my résumé that I can help answer?' This ensured that if there were any hesitancy about my qualifications or experience, they said it out loud, and I had a chance to answer and leave the interview on a good note."

Another trick Daniela used in her own interviews is something I find very effective, too: adjusting your demeanor based on the person who's interviewing you.

She remembers: "If it was someone in the news department, I knew to have at least five major news stories I'd been following in my back pocket, so that I could dish out common talking points whenever possible. In my interview with *Saturday Night Live*, I knew it was a laid-back culture, so I tried to be a little more relaxed in my demeanor and more conversational.

"I've always found that mimicking the demeanor of the person interviewing you will help you resonate more: Are they speaking slowly or at a rapid pace? Loud or softly? Do they appear relaxed or more professional? I tried to be aware of my environment and use their cues to adjust my tone and movements as much as possible."

> I've always found that mimicking the demeanor of the person interviewing you will help you resonate more.
> —DANIELA PIERRE-BRAVO

This is knowing your audience and adjusting yourself to communicate effectively in a way that the person in front of you sees immediately.

From early on in her time at NBC, Daniela has interviewed hundreds of young people who go on to work for us, from interns to the NBC pages who rotate in and out of *Morning Joe*. Self-awareness is one of the big things she looks for in interviews.

"In order to be effective in all areas of the job, we need interns and entry-level assistants who have a strong sense of what they bring to the table, and how they fit into the ever-changing environment—whether they're running around during the live show or adapting to the office hours afterward. They should have a sense of when to take charge of a situation and make decisions vs. when they just need to put their head down and do the work."

As Daniela knows, it's important for our interns and production assistants to grasp the urgency of their tasks and to be meticulous about how they complete them. She adds, "Whether it's errand running, getting coffee, printing scripts, or running them to set for our show hosts, the assistants and interns need to be professional and to maintain a great attitude (because the worst thing is to have a grumpy intern greet our television guests at the crack of dawn, while the sun is rising). With our early hours, it's important to appear alert and approachable."

Being able to function well as part of a group is also essential. Daniela asks the following questions to help evaluate prospective candidates:

"In a work group setting, what role are you most comfortable playing? What is the adjective you'd use to describe yourself when working in groups?"

The answer usually falls somewhere among the "leader," someone who calls the shots; someone who supports the leader (the person who's head-down working to get something done); or the devil's advocate of the group, who brings up ideas that seem out of the ordinary, or even contradictory, to make an end result stronger and more sustainable.

She explains, "I pay close attention to how they categorize themselves and why. It usually gives me a good idea of their experience working in groups, and whether they're effective problem-solvers."

Daniela is trying to evaluate whether the prospective candidate is self aware enough to know when to stay in his or her lane vs. when they need to take the initiative if need be. Both are important skills.

Overall, the candidates who knock it out of the park are self-aware enough to know why the job is likely to be a good fit, and always have questions and answers prepared. They come looking as if they're ready to do the job.

Another common question asked in interviews is "Why do you want this job?"

This one may sound pretty easy, but there are lots of different ways to answer it.

"One sure way to go *un*noticed is by answering that question from the perspective of what the job can do for you," Daniela explains. "For example, I have had tons of prospective candidates answer this way: 'I want this job because I really like the fast pace of it all. I like not being at my desk. I prefer to run around. And being in a live studio environment seems like an amazing opportunity.'"

Before answering, stop and think about why anyone would ask you this. Yes, the interviewer does want to know that you're enthusiastic about the job. However, even more important, they want to know what you can add to the job. This goes back to Cal Newport's point about thinking from the company's perspective.

Show that you are aware of the organization's needs. What can YOU bring to the table?

If you fail to add that element to the answer, you may be losing out on a valuable opportunity to stand out.

Donny Deutsch, a regular on *Morning Joe* and chairman of the multibillion-dollar advertising agency Deutsch Inc. encourages anyone who is interviewing to bring what he has coined the "hungry eye."

"It starts in the eyes. I'm looking for the person who's looking to prove something beyond the job."

Bring eagerness and fire to communicating why you are the right fit—but you also want to show that you can play well with others.

At the end of the day, Donny says, "I look for good human beings. I don't get seduced by pure talent because there are enough people in the world that are wildly talented and also really decent human beings. That's what makes a workplace work."

> It starts in the eyes. I'm looking for the person who's looking to prove something beyond the job.
>
> —DONNY DEUTSCH

One of the most valuable skills a young professional can cultivate is the ability to connect—whether it's with prospective employers, people you meet out networking, or potential career mentors and allies.

The Power of Connection

I asked Joanna Coles, former chief content officer for Hearst Magazines and former editor in chief of *Cosmopolitan* magazine, to share her ideas on the topic. She has hired and fired the best of them and has a keen eye for what makes an effective communicator, having overseen one of the biggest millennial female media brands in the world.

In Joanna's view, it comes down to this: "The ones who are succeeding are the ones who have emotional intelligence, are good at dealing with people, and have advanced tech skills."

Luckily, your generation has the digital nativism thing down; but the emotional fluency part is something that takes work. And unlike technical skills, soft skills, like the ability to listen or show empathy, are not often taught. Sadly, social media can make them even harder to finesse.

Joanna Coles credits her emotional fluency at the beginning of her career to asking questions and having an immense curiosity, which drew her into actual face-to-face conversations. Part of the learning experience, Joanna says, is that you don't have the chance to really control how things go.

"Pauses are awkward; sometimes you can say the wrong thing, sometimes you talk over each other, and it's embarrassing. But the more you do it, the more fluent you become and the more you learn. And I think the more you listen, the more you hear, the more you learn. And the better business you do."

Say you put yourself out there and things are going badly: you're trying to make small talk and the person you are talking to is giving you nothing back. Radio silence. Things are just plain awkward. Joanna suggests the following: "Ask questions."

Show curiosity. "Usually people will begin to unload. Everybody has at least one story that they want to tell."

The next best thing you can do is to be prepared: do advance research and take advantage of the tools technology gives you.

Joanna adds: "You can always go in being super-prepared because often it's just a search of Wikipedia or a quick flick through Google Search. When you go in that way, you're not starting from scratch, you're already starting at two out of ten and then learning.

"Some people find it easier than others to talk, but asking questions, listening, and then asking another question, is a matter of practice. You'll talk to a whole array of people, and you'll begin to see who's good at it and then copy them. Look at their mannerisms: how do successful people get to be successful? There's no shame in plagiarizing their skills. Don't plagiarize their words, but do plagiarize their skills."

Joanna has a checklist that can help you communicate more effectively.

- A straightforward handshake
- Eye contact throughout a conversation
- Not only asking how someone is, but also listening and responding to what they are saying in real time.
- Remembering details from a previous conversation you've had. Maybe they've just come back from vacation or had a sick family member.

Joanna also suggests using every early experience as a learning opportunity: "It's paying attention to how you behave and how you feel before and after a meeting that might be important to you. Keep notes: Did you do this well, did you come out of this feeling like you'd learned something? Or did you feel that you made an ass of yourself? What could you do differently to make it better the next time, or at least to come out without feeling like you've scolded yourself?

"When you leave a meeting or finish a conversation, what do you think the other person took away from you? Were they one of those people who coerced you into saying more than you should have said? Did they get more out of the meeting than you did? What was the balance in this meeting?

"Keeping notes and understanding that most meetings are a transaction is very helpful. And interestingly, they don't really teach you these skill sets in school."

Knowing how to connect and make positive impressions by the way you carry yourself and communicate are all things you should use to your advantage. This is especially important when you're meeting someone new, following up with a new contact, and interviewing. You have to find a way to resonate with them. Give them a reason to remember you, and set up that follow-up call or additional interview.

> **Keeping notes and understanding that most meetings are a transaction is very helpful. And interestingly, they don't really teach you these skill sets in school.**
> —JOANNA COLES

Your Online Presence

Just as important as your personal presentation is your digital persona. Nowadays, whether it's your voice mail, email signature, or social media handles, you're really out there—all of you! Take into careful consideration how you are being projected in the digital space, whether you're networking, or especially if you're job hunting!

Some things to keep in mind to make sure you are presenting yourself professionally and not getting in the way of your message:

- Go through your Twitter feed to see if the conversations you're in online accurately represent your point of view. Is there anything that a potential job lead, or boss, could look at with disapproval or take the wrong way? Stay away from anything that is provocative or might be offensive to others.

- Keep your Instagram and Facebook handles private and think about what you post. Again, bosses, recruiters, potential job leads, and people you network with HAVE ACCESS TO ALL OF THIS AND WILL USE IT. Stay on the safe side and put the phone down after you've started drinking!

- Are your profile pictures up to date? They're the first thing that comes up on a Google search. Make sure they send the right message! Think about taking a clean head shot, especially for platforms like LinkedIn, which is strictly professional.

- Everything, even the way you construct your emails, should be given a second look to ensure it has the right tone to represent you professionally. This includes your email signature line. Make sure it makes you look mature and professional. And watch the exclamation points in the body of your emails. You don't want an email filled with !!!!!, especially if you are corresponding with someone in a senior role.

Following Up

Just as important as making a good first impression is developing that contact.

Making sure you follow up with your contacts, whether it's someone you met at an informational or at a network event, is key to building a relationship with that person. Make a plan to keep in touch. For example, after meeting someone, reach back out within twenty-four hours, and send a handwritten card or an email to make yourself memorable.

For fashion designer Rebecca Minkoff, the follow-up was an important way to nurture and maintain her business contacts. It proved to be incredibly effective in growing her network in a meaningful way. Whenever Rebecca was introduced to people in her industry, she asked for business cards. They became her currency.

She notes, "At the end of the night, I would go home and count my business cards. They became more valuable than money. I would think about how many business cards I got, and I would always follow up with a nice note and ask the person for coffee or a drink. I would always find a way to meet them."

Making sure you check in with your contacts is important, too. "I casually kept in touch, always pretending that each outreach was the first time, never getting frustrated if someone didn't reply, and just kind of constantly reminding them that I was there," Rebecca says.

It's important to remember to not get frustrated when leads or follow-up emails go unanswered. It's a lot like fishing, Rebecca points out: some work out and some don't. You have to keep going and focus on those relationships that stick. Don't get discouraged when an email or note goes unanswered.

> You have to keep going and focus on those relationships that stick. Don't get discouraged when an email or note goes unanswered.
>
> —REBECCA MINKOFF

Joanna Coles observes: "You have to listen; you have to hear the cues. You're listening for key words, and that's how you become fluent in the language of relationships. Millennials and Generation Z have just had less exposure to it."

RECAP: Nailing the Interview and Making Lasting Impressions

- Look the part but don't overdo it. Simple is always better. Look and feel comfortable above all.
- The first interview is not the place to make a daring style choice.
- André Leon Talley style tip: Look neat, presentable, and well-mannered. Inner confidence shines through more than any designer wear.
- Project confidence with good posture. Sit up, abs in, shoulders back.
- Self-awareness and an understanding of your audience should show through with every answer.

- Bring the "hungry eye."
- Body language musts: have a strong handshake, make eye contact, respond in real time, feel out and adjust to the energy of the person/room.
- CONNECT and RESONATE.

CHAPTER FOUR

NAVIGATING YOUR EARLY CAREER

You've made it through the interview and showcased your desire for the job—and now you have it. The real work begins! There is so much ahead of you to learn and take in. These first few jobs are critical for your personal development. It's time to really understand how to earn your value, and then grow it.

But in today's world of work, you face some fresh challenges.

When I started out in television in my 20s as an intern and then a production assistant, the lanes in the workplace were a bit clearer. Everyone around me was about the same age as me. Today, you may be working alongside people of all ages, from many different backgrounds. Right off the bat, young women have to handle workplace situations that require maturity. Learning how to communicate and connect, understanding the expectations of the job, and figuring out how and when to assert yourself can be confusing.

Young people want to figure out their big-picture career goals right away, which can muddle their sense of worth and create a distorted perception of purpose. Most of you starting out don't know exactly what you want to do. And that's okay! Your 20s are for learning, exploring, and gathering workplace experiences of all kinds.

The nitty-gritty of those first jobs can be used to your advantage: growing your network, learning how to navigate your environment, and building trust and respect from those around you. As young women, you need to take the time to grow.

With the Mark Zuckerbergs and Sophia Amorusos held up as role models in the workplace, it's easy for millennials to feel like they're behind—even before they've begun.

Dwelling too much on the big picture can be distracting. It undermines the progress you need in the short term to grow into your career. Your first few years are great chances to learn, make mistakes, recover from them, build resilience, and learn about yourself along the way. That's how you find your bearings. You can't figure out your entire career when you're just starting out. Embrace the twists and turns that come with finding your way!

It's great to be ambitious and have your own goals—please, be ambitious! If you're working around me, you have to be; that's how you bring your greatest qualities to the table.

But ambition is not just "I wanna get to the top!" It's "I want to grow," "I want to have a full life," "I want to be really good at what I do." Then you need to develop the skills to help you reach those goals. It's all about continuously developing and growing your value. Ambition requires grit, determination, and a powerful work ethic.

Establishing Your Brand

As you're navigating the beginning of your career, you'll find that the things you contribute in the office, plus your overall attitude, will become an extension of you. The value you add, and the skill sets you develop, will translate to your professional brand. Though it takes patience and diligence to develop one, a personal brand will help you resonate with your coworkers, especially your boss.

Ultimately your professional brand is a robust and polished personal narrative. Focus groups we conducted with Harvard's polling director confirmed that this is recognized as one of the most important aspects of a post-college career. Because it's so important! And it took me some time to really own mine.

Looking back at my 22-year-old self, I can see that my professional brand was vastly different than it is now. It took me a while to be comfortable with myself; I spent too much time focusing on building up the physical. My 22-year-old self really wanted to look like a beauty queen, and she really didn't understand her value and her beauty.

In meetings I was usually sweating bullets. I was uncomfortable in my own skin, uncomfortable in my clothes, and definitely uncomfortable with my hair. And all those things distracted me. I was not my best, and it took me twenty years to really figure out who I was, what I wanted to be, how I wanted to look and feel. It took me all those years to learn to communicate effectively who I was in the workplace.

At 22, my brand would have been: scrappy, eager, ready to work and learn, and willing to do anything to get my foot in the door. My brand was a description of what I brought to the table; it was made of the things that defined me. It was a way to show my professional marketability, which was of course limited then. And you know what? Pretending that I was contributing any more would have been a lie. It would have been misinformation. Selling yourself for more than you can offer puts you in a terrible position. An entry-level job is an entry-level job—it's fine to be eager but untested.

When I was in my mid-20s I was starting out as a reporter in Hartford, Connecticut, covering politics and crime. The building blocks were expanding. By the time I was in my late 20s, I was a TV reporter and a news host who covered whatever happened in or around the town. My brand at that time was just that: "local reporter in Hartford."

My advice for the time you are starting out: before being known for a lot of different things, make sure you can do one thing really well and then grow from there.

Is your brand that you're a problem-solver? That you're eager? Hungry to learn? Great! Don't overstate or oversell it. Your brand will evolve. It will never stay the same. It will grow. But when you are starting out, make it true. It can start as a description of yourself, and then as you get your first jobs under your belt, it can be what you do: the responsibilities you take on, the value you've brought to an organization.

If your professional brand is being a "hard worker" or being "organized" or "creative," SHOW that you are those things through your actions. Look for opportunities that strengthen and expand that persona.

Daniela has been able to evolve her brand dramatically from the start of her career working with me. Early on, her brand would have been "persistent and scrappy."

She was always the one who found a solution to a problem, found a "yes" to a "no," and did it all with professionalism and attention to detail. Whether it was convincing a hard-to-get show guest to come on the show, or solving logistical issues, she was on it. Organically, that became part of her brand, her professional persona. And any time I had a difficult task, or I needed to rely on someone to get something done, she was the first person I thought of. That is the power of branding: the ability to resonate.

More people are eager to hire someone scrappy and eager to work than someone who had a lot to say about themselves at age 21. Unless you've built a fully functioning business by then, there's not much more to add.

Building a personal brand takes the same type of focus and dedication that it takes to build a business: it can take years of putting in the work. Focus on developing your skill set, and you'll get there.

Your First Jobs Will Not Be Your Dream Jobs

Members of a focus group conducted by Harvard Kennedy School's Institute of Politics for this book noted that millennials have a hard time recognizing if they're in a place at work that will ultimately pay off. Daniela, who helped with these interviews alongside Harvard pollster John Della Volpe, notes: "For many in my generation the fear is: 'What if I'm losing time doing one thing when I could potentially be doing something else that could be more beneficial and rewarding?' It's the fear of dedicating yourself to a job that will take you nowhere."

Young women who don't have a firm understanding of what they want to do experience more anxiety because their path is unclear. It sounds counterintuitive, but the truth is, having too many opportunities can cause inertia. An emphasis on finding "the perfect fit" right out of school puts a tremendous amount of pressure on young people and causes anxiety.

I asked actress and producer Eva Longoria about this desire to get ahead quickly, and she underscored the value of starting at the bottom: "In the [business] world, there's a hierarchy, and it's good to start from the bottom and work your way up. I think it's so important in any industry to touch every rung of the ladder, so that once you're at the top, you know why you're there, and you never lose your footing."

In the [business] world, there's a hierarchy, and it's good to start from the bottom and work your way up. I think it's so important in any industry to touch every rung of the ladder, so that once you're at the top, you know why you're there, and you never lose your footing.

—EVA LONGORIA

Eva is certainly a household name now, but she started in small roles. By the time she started her company and started directing and producing, she knew every job beneath her.

In Hollywood, Eva says, the get-famous-quick mentality is pure fantasy: "I feel sometimes with millennials they want to jump to the top. If you're talking about Hollywood, they want to be discovered at Starbucks! And that's not the case. You have to work your way up in any industry."

> There's a systemic impatience, thanks, in large part, to social media and technology.
> —SIMON SINEK

The idea that your first few jobs should feel like a great fit is a myth. Simon Sinek, optimist and bestselling author, observes: "Technology has made us all more impatient with everything in our lives. Think about how impatient we get when our friends don't get back to us. You send a text and don't get a reply immediately—you check and check and check. I think this isn't unique to millennials. There's a systemic impatience, thanks, in large part, to social media and technology.

"For people growing up like this, there's an intense sense of impatience in their careers that if I don't nail it, I will waste time and lose out. I get that a lot when I talk to young people. That may be one of the reasons they are hard to lead."

Here's the bottom line on framing your early career: in your 20s, when you're less likely to have family, and more likely to have lower expenses and more freedom, use that time to try to figure out what your cause may truly be, and what your passions are. Your 20s are a valuable time to be junior and to learn. Sinek encourages people in their 20s to "show up as a student knowing you know very little, instead of pretending to know everything when you know nothing at all. We all know you don't, because you have one year of experience in the workforce. It doesn't matter how smart you are; it's a simple equation of experience."

The truth is, it's *very* likely that your first job will not be your dream job. And your second or third probably won't be, either. It's all about exposure to the world of work and learning as you go.

Cal Newport, associate professor at Georgetown University and author of *So Good They Can't Ignore You* and *Deep Work*, has written extensively about the anxiety and chronic job-hopping associated with millennials. He goes as far as to say that the idea you're meant to do only one thing professionally is largely a myth.

He observes that if you start in the workplace with a "follow your passion" mentality, you're likely to set yourself up for failure, job-hopping, and constant worry that your current work situation isn't the one you were meant to inhabit.

Cal has asked people from a range of different industries about their career journeys. For this book, he recalls what he found: "One of the striking things I learned was that most of these people who have a passion for their work did not start off with it.... This idea that you're wired to do something, and once you discover this passion and match it to a job, you're going to feel great, you're going to feel engaged, you're going to feel purposeful, is largely a myth. Your passion tends to develop over time. It's something people cultivate, not something that they start with."

The "passion" mind-set in approaching work can be dangerous, he says, because it's characterized by the belief that your job owes you something: What does this job offer me? Young people afflicted with it constantly ask themselves if they love their jobs, or repeatedly compare their job to others, and wonder if they might love that other job more. It's a losing game.

Number one, you feel like you're in a dead-end job? Well, most likely you're not. Your current experience has value, even if it's a bad experience, and even if you don't get along with the people you work with. Because at the end of the day you are learning something, which is important.

Simon Sinek adds: "My first boss was one of the worst bosses I've ever had. I realized I could quit or learn how not to lead like this person. On a team of six people, I learned how we took care of each other. I learned how to network. I learned how to put up with stress. It was one of the most valuable experiences of my life. We don't learn much when things are going right. We learn the most when things go wrong, and an imperfect job is a fantastic place to learn.

"And here's the news flash: no job is perfect. There is no point in going from job to job to job looking for the lottery. 'The one' doesn't exist. There's always a honeymoon."

Cal Newport proposes an alternative that may feel counterintuitive. Try to cultivate a mind-set in which you are constantly asking yourself the following questions: What value am I offering to this job or organization? How hard would I be to replace? How can I become more valuable? How can I develop additional skills to become more valuable?

We don't learn much when things are going right. We learn the most when things go wrong, and an imperfect job is a fantastic place to learn.

—SIMON SINEK

In the first five years of your career, your goal should be to develop a craft.

He advises: "Learn to do something rare and valuable; learn how to do it well. No one really enjoys being an apprentice, but you do it. And once you learn the skills of the apprenticeship, it can be deeply satisfying. I often use career satisfaction through this lens of skills. If you develop more skills, it gives you more control over your career. And it's that control that might lead you into something that becomes a deep source of passion."

Cal gives an example: "Look at professional athletes, musicians, and chess players, whose craft is demonstrably all that matters. And if you look at how professional athletes, musicians, and chess players get better, you'll notice they don't do the same thing, over and over again. They deliberately practice. They say, 'Where can I get better? How can I design practices that push me to get better at what I do?'

"If you watch a professional guitar player practice, they're not just sitting there playing riffs and having fun; it's a really hard thing they are doing, pushing themselves out of their comfort zone to get better. You should be doing the same type of deliberate practice in your own career. You should be identifying useful skills you don't have and stretching yourself.

"Give yourself exercises that encourage you to learn new things—hard things. You can't just expect that if you work hard, but do the same thing over and over again, you'll get better. Getting better requires focused practice. You have to think like a professional athlete, musician, or chess player. What can I design that's going to make me better than I am now?"

As Cal suggests, hone your craft. Figure out your point of advantage.

Asking "Is this what I am meant to do?" right out of the gate is going to distract you from really focusing on the opportunities to grow in those first jobs.

Donny Deutsch works with dozens of millennials and has observed their innate need not only to get ahead quickly, but also to feel the need to make change, to disrupt an industry, to feel that their ideas are in some way revolutionary. But, he points out, before you can disrupt the system, you have to learn the rules to the system.

In my conversations with Donny, he observes that a lot of young professionals, many of them very smart kids, run into a wall five and six years out of college. They stumble and don't know what they want to do next, because they came straight out of college thinking they could build their first app or run a business out of thin air. They come out with guns blazing but with little foundation.

"Nobody wants just that first job, because they read about the Evan Spiegels and the 24-year-old guys who are worth 74 billion dollars," Donny says.

The problem with this? It's unrealistic. It's an outlier scenario. "It's an unreal ideal," he adds.

So how do you compensate and leverage playing by the rules while also making an impact?

Donny's advice is that no matter what your first work experience or job is, whether you work in TV or in advertising, you need to take a step back, breathe, and really take a moment to understand what you're there to do in those first few years.

"You're there just learning how to interact in the workplace, how to talk to people in business-speak, how to write a memo, how to get along in a world of commerce and business. And the mistake that young people make is when they go, 'No, I don't want to work at a company my whole life, so I'm not going to go work at a company.'"

Basic, fundamental human interaction in a commercial workplace is what you are there to learn in the first few years of your job.

"It doesn't matter if you're working at an insurance company and are not going to do insurance eventually. You're learning about sales, you're learning about human interactions, you're learning 'I have to do this to get that.' If you're learning about motivation, you're learning about structure, and about consequence," Donny adds.

Even young professionals who are iconoclasts or just want to go their own way can be really successful if they can manage, as

Donny says, to "plug in and play" for a while. Donny argues that it can be incredibly important to learn the ropes and the fabric of a business infrastructure—especially before you go out and do your own thing, if that's your goal.

He remembers talking to a friend's young adult son, who was struggling two years into the workforce. This young man was a self-proclaimed "disrupter" in the business world.

But first, there have to be rules in place to disrupt. With whole-hearted frustration, Donny told him: "How do you know what to disrupt?! You don't even know what the f*** is out there!"

In the fast-paced, highly creative advertising world Donny knows so well, he finds that all young people "want to be disrupters." But here is the question he (too frequently) finds himself asking millennials: "Until you know what the status quo is on some level, how do you know how to disrupt anything?"

Donny tells me about another experience with a young man who was in his second year of work out of college: "This kid says to me, 'I'm a branding guy.'"

To which, without censor, Donny responded: "What do you mean you're a branding guy? You just graduated college, you don't even know what the f*** a brand is!"

It's great to come out into the workplace with a need to be part of a greater purpose. This is one of the things that makes your generation so important for the future of the workplace, and that will change the way we do business for the greater good.

When you're starting out, it's best to assume you're still learning. It's okay to get there and not know all the answers! There is nothing wrong with acknowledging that your skill and experience level are different than that of other people in your workplace.

Simon Sinek says: "The people who took the time to perfect their skills and gain experience in their 20s become vastly more effective executives, vastly more effective as leaders, and quite frankly, they do much better financially when they hit their 30s. Because if you jump from job to job to job, you might make money more quickly, but then you cap out and don't learn much."

You may have to try any number of career choices before you find a place where you feel at home in the workplace—even if that doesn't happen in your first few jobs. As Facebook COO Sheryl Sandberg puts it: "Your career is a jungle gym, it's not a linear path."

Applying These Lessons IRL

Anjali Sud, who became CEO of Vimeo at 34 years old, emphasizes the importance of understanding that a career may zig and zag: "At a young age, I aspired to be a business leader. And to be the best business leader I could be, I sought to develop a broad and diverse skill set. I thought that being well-versed in financials and analytics would enable me to be more effective in business. I also thought that a quantitative background would allow me to overcome potential subjectivity and bias in my career down the line. One of the most objective measures of business success is to be able to understand how you impacted a company's profit-and-loss statement."

So as she looked ahead, she decided to go into investment banking. But after four years of school—like me—she couldn't get a job. Even after going to the Wharton School at the University of Pennsylvania, one of the best business schools in the country, she was rejected by every bank to which she applied. She recalls, "I was about to graduate, and I didn't have a job. I was very dejected from all the 'nos,' especially when it felt like all my classmates were getting these great jobs at brand-name firms."

Ultimately, she got scrappy and creative, and found a start-up investment bank that had just opened and was looking for its first analyst. Nobody had ever heard of it.

Though she got the job, she still felt she'd failed by not going to a large firm: "I was convinced that my career was over before it started—that I wouldn't be able to accomplish my dream of running a company because I didn't check the boxes right out of college. But my experience at this start-up investment bank turned out to be a great one, that truly prepared me for my future path by giving me opportunities to own projects I never would have gotten at a traditional firm. It is now so clear to me that there's no set formula to achieve your dreams. You don't have to go to Goldman Sachs or hit every milestone to ultimately make the impact you want on the world."

Her clear message to young people starting out is the same as mine: "You're empowered at every step of your career to change your path, to create your own opportunities. You're not held back by whatever's happened in the past. I never would have believed that in my 20s. It's something I believe now."

Take Laura Brown, editor in chief of *InStyle* and former executive editor at *Harper's Bazaar*. She got her foot in the door by working and reporting for a publication called *Australian Family*, whose content was all parenting-oriented—not exactly the content she was interested in or excited to create as "a young, hustling 19-year-old who liked skirts," she tells me. The girl had a thing for fashion early on! But at the end of the day it was her first reporting job, and it was great experience.

Laura took a job she didn't necessarily love, but it helped her get her feet wet in the field; and it gave her time to understand what she really wanted to do. By doing her job, and doing it well, she was able to leverage her interest in writing.

Finally, she landed a job in her desired field, fashion, working in production at a magazine called *Mode*: "It fancied itself like *W*—a sort of Sydney social magazine. I would chase people around with a clipboard, saying, 'Where's your text?' on time, and then having to handwrite them, photocopy, and revise them maybe fifteen times."

What she really wanted to do was write, so she raised her hand any chance she got, writing pieces for the "funny fashion print page" after work and in the mornings. Eventually she had enough grounding and recognition to become a features editor.

For young women trying to make it in the industry of their choice, she has a few words of advice: "Enthusiasm and ability are the two greatest characteristics anybody can have, especially when you're younger and just in the door. You've got to communicate that you're happy to be there—that you're just getting going and have your whole future ahead of you. Go to every event. Go to whatever you need to. You have to be fed by the industry you want to succeed in; you empower yourself by the experience of working with others within it—and by showing up."

Kasie Hunt, NBC Capitol Hill correspondent and host of MSNBC's *Kasie DC*, admits that she only learned the value of her first job later in her career. She was frustrated as an editorial assistant at the AP wire service, "the oldest of old-school places to be a journalist," as she describes it.

"Seniority is respected more than anything. My first six months in the job they basically treated me like a glorified typist, because I sat behind whoever was the main White House reporter, typically somebody who had a couple decades of experience. My job would basically be to type as fast as I possibly could, so they could hand in copy that was as complete as possible. I knew how to type really fast. I learned how to type in the seventh grade, which turned out to be the most important skill I had. The job felt like drudgery. I wasn't where I needed to be: I wanted to move up.

> You have to be fed by the industry you want to succeed in; you empower yourself by the experience of working with others within it—and by showing up.
> —LAURA BROWN

"But what I learned to do on the wire, which was to sit there and type as fast as you can and then listen for the most important thing, is something that I do literally every day. And that training was something I completely underestimated. I got to sit behind the best people in the industry and learn how to do it, which was awesome, even if I didn't see it at the time."

Josh Earnest, former White House press secretary for President Obama, found that the menial tasks he did at the beginning of his career had a direct correlation to the type of work he would eventually do as communications director for the White House.

Right out of college, Josh had an opportunity to take an unpaid position in a campaign during Houston's mayoral race. Also working a side job to support his small role in the campaign, he stood out by becoming indispensable to his team, even if that meant doing unglamorous work.

"At the beginning, I was not entrusted with a lot of responsibility," he tells us. His role was to piece together physical newspaper clippings and organize them for the campaign's opposition research department. In the days before the Internet, when you couldn't easily copy, paste, and print, Josh had to go through each physical article.

"I spent literally weeks getting newsprint all over my hands… unfolding these things trying to make them fit on the eight-and-a-half-inch pieces of paper, shrinking down the size of the newsprint so it would fit, or cutting it and pasting it in different forms."

Although it was grunt work, it taught Josh a few important lessons. "People saw that I was willing to work hard, even when it wasn't glamorous, even when people weren't paying attention. It was frustrating, and it was hard work, but there was an appreciation for that kind of work ethic."

That attitude and work ethic made him indispensable to the team he worked for. Suddenly, he was the most informed person in the room about what the press was saying about his boss.

"I knew more about what was in those clips, and I knew more about his history, than anybody else on the staff. That turned me into a genuine resource.

"Later, as we were working to defend his record in law enforcement, I had this knowledge built up from standing at that photocopy machine and reading those stories, and then being responsible for filing them by subject area. That helped make the argument that he was a good police chief and helped defend his record in the face of some controversies. It made me a resource in the campaign, not just as somebody who is willing to work hard, but somebody who built up an expertise in something that became very valuable to the candidate and to the rest of the campaign."

Getting the menial tasks done right can work as a vehicle to advancement. Retired Admiral William McRaven observed in an often-quoted 2014 commencement speech at the University of Texas, which became the bestselling book *Make Your Bed: Little Things That Can Change Your Life…and Maybe the World*, "It's a lot about teamwork. We used to have a saying in combat: Your proximity to the fight was not your value to the organization. I don't care if you're an analyst working in the United States. Just because you're not the SEAL or Ranger in the fight, you're still of incredible value to the guys and gals in the battlefield."

...nailing the details on even the most tedious jobs—is an invest-
ment, and a window of opportunity for the big responsibilities.

When you get the small things right, you're showing dedication to the team. Most important, you're gaining *trust,* and
showing that your boss and your coworkers can count on you.
Making your bed every day—nailing the details on even the most
tedious jobs—is an investment, and a window of opportunity
for the big responsibilities.

Dia Simms, president of Combs Enterprises, also emphasizes
that one person's dirty work may be another person's way to
get ahead: "The CEO Genome Project shows that there are
three particular subsets of behaviors that drive the likelihood
of becoming what they call a 'CEO sprinter.' One of them is
finding the project that nobody wants to do because you don't
have to fight for it and they'll be happy you volunteered for it.
Take leadership. Kill it. Any improvement will be viewed as a
win. Put measurable wins on the board as early and as often
as you can.

"As an example, at Combs Enterprises, we had a ridiculous
amount of footage that needed to be digitized and optimized.
We have a young executive who volunteered, took it on, and
ended up being promoted as a result."

"This puts you in the spotlight, and makes you known as a
problem-solver."

Emily Jane Fox, a 29-year-old staff writer at *Vanity Fair,* and
author of *Born Trump: Inside America's First Family* (Harper
Collins, 2018) has found great success by putting in the grunt

work to get started in journalism, and by being okay with not loving every aspect of the first job she had.

"Undergrad, I studied creative writing and politics, and then I went straight to Columbia Journalism. I took classes with professors who were at the places where I wanted to work; I was very strategic."

At a job fair at the school, she met representatives from five media companies, chosen at random. After doing "an insane amount of research on each publication," she proposed five stories she thought would go well on each company's website. Because she was super-prepared, she wound up getting four job offers: "I got an offer from CNN that day and took it. It was crazy; I started five days after I graduated."

She started in business reporting, not an area she had a ton of experience in. "I covered labor and minimum wage, and markets I had no idea about in all sorts of different areas: retail, Walmart, McDonald's, all sorts of companies, all mixed up, which is a great thing for your first job."

For Emily, knowing that that first job wasn't going to be her forever job, but rather a way in, made her even better at it. She knew that she would eventually be writing and reporting on things that were more in line with her interests, but she also understood the importance of raising her hand and paying her dues in order to get that initial seat at the table. The rest will follow.

"With every job you take, there are going to be sacrifices; it's not going to be exactly what you want. Sometimes covering markets meant that, for five weeks at a time, I had to get to work at 5 a.m. to cover European markets, something I knew nothing about. I would have to call traders there and ask, 'Can you tell me why the market dipped three points at the end of the day?'"

She advanced in her chosen field by saying a loud yes (!) to all the opportunities that came her way, which is a great way to build your value—even if you don't want to, and it's not exactly glamorous. It shows your boss—or in Emily's case, her editor—that you can take one for the team.

She explains how her willingness has helped her career: "It has benefited me to say, 'Yeah, I'll work the weekend shift, I'll work the 5 a.m. shift. You want me to fly to Chicago for a way to write that story, even though it's horrible because I have to be back in Chicago three days later?'…I just say yes. Because then I'm thought of as a valuable team member." And she has been. She's made herself, at a young age, an irreplaceable teammate, which pays off when it's time for a review: "If you're someone they want to keep, you have leverage."

> **Building that trust means knowing when to say "no," and meaning it when you say "yes."**
> —DIA SIMMS

Dia Simms also points out that you can make a strong impression by exhibiting the old-fashioned virtues of stability and reliability: "Just do what you say you're going to do. I get that it sounds very simple, but to me this is a real virtue. If you are the person who says 'yes' and then actually always does what you say you will do, you're enormously valuable. You're establishing a trust footprint with the person you're dealing with."

She adds: "Building that trust means knowing when to say 'no,' and meaning it when you say 'yes.'"

Dia's point is reinforced by Patricia Langer, former EVP of human resources at NBCUniversal, who encourages millennials to think about expanding their scope of responsibilities. She stresses that it's okay to make mistakes, and to ask for help: "Another stereotype about millennials is they all have helicopter parents; that they're very dependent on their parents. In the workplace, you don't have your parents there. You're on your own. So it's okay to take a little bit of risk. It's okay to want to grow by thinking about areas that you may not be as strong in and trying to learn how to master those areas. But millennials really need to learn how to do it on their own: to be resourceful and to be independent."

So how does a generation that is so purpose-driven stay energized as they enter the workforce, knowing their purpose may take time to formulate, and their first jobs may not feel rewarding? Admittedly, this can be discouraging to hear if you are a millennial eager and itching to get your career started.

Donny's advice to young people is: "Always go for your dream. Do it your way. Always find something that in some way, shape, or form is your own thing so that you're not beholden to any great infrastructure. But plug in for a while so you at least understand what basic business interaction is like."

Donny has been able to create a very successful business for himself now, but he had to start with small steps like everyone else: "I remember my first job at Ogilvy, a big advertising agency. In those first eighteen months of my career, I learned how to dress, how to talk, and how to deal with a different authoritative structure. You have to learn how to communicate differently from the way you're used to. You have to learn to communicate to someone you're competing with. The closest thing to competition was people who were taking tests together, but it wasn't a zero-sum game."

It may seem elementary, but being able to talk to someone easily, to engage the person you are speaking with, takes time to learn. This is especially true in the workplace, where there are so many styles of communicating. You need to understand how to engage. And it's getting harder and harder to do when the majority of our live conversations are being replaced by electronic communications.

CHAPTER FIVE

OWNING YOUR VOICE AND COMMUNICATING EFFECTIVELY

If you're just entering the workforce, your competitive advantage, right off the bat, is your digital savviness. It's your second language; you just get it. It's your not-so-secret weapon. We now live in an online world, and millennials and the generation that follows are the most comfortable in this habitat.

BUT, that said, an online world doesn't give you a whole lot of opportunity to interact with others *in person*. You can't finesse a job interview on a cell phone! You need to read the reactions of the people speaking with you and understand their tone. You have to learn to communicate not only verbally, but also be able to pick up nonverbal cues and body language.

Yes, digital nativism is a critical skill, but it can affect your ability to make meaningful connections around you in more subtle ways. In this chapter I want to explore the ways that being tech-dependent—not just tech-savvy—can hamper your career, and what you can do about it.

To take your career to the next level, you have to be able to communicate successfully in any setting. Using your voice effectively is critical to moving ahead—which is why it's a fundamental pillar of my Know Your Value message.

To create real relationships, you have to start using your voice—your physical voice. People need to hear its sound.

One of the most important things you can do for yourself is work on your voice. And you'll hear me talk about it in many sections in this book. Using your voice effectively means not only feeling comfortable in your own skin and presenting yourself confidently with physical tools—great posture, focused eye contact, and so on. It means speaking to people in person, and being aware of the need to speak clearly, concisely, and calmly in a professional setting.

Being aware of the sound of your voice will help you get a message across when you need to. You will be able to speak out in public confidently and state your case when it matters most—in advocating for yourself and negotiating.

My coauthor practiced this trick from early on and it proved really useful. As an 18-year-old, petite woman, Daniela found that working on her physical voice and using a lower register every time she spoke to clients in her Mary Kay business made her appear more mature, knowledgeable, and professional. She found this tip on YouTube!

"I followed other successful consultants and picked up physical mannerism and ways of speaking in public, one of which was to speak in a lower voice. I was always worried about clients I'd just met at a presentation who were often older than me, thinking, 'Who is this little girl?' So when I was trying to get my start in the media industry, I modulated my voice to help build confidence as I was interviewing. I still use that trick today whenever I do presentations or speak in front of an audience."

This is EXACTLY what I mean when I say to use your voice effectively! This is what worked for Daniela; you might find that you can modulate your voice in different ways to feel more powerful when you speak. Find ways to project your voice and get your point across with poise and maturity. You've got to practice!

One of the most frustrating things I've encountered with young professionals who work for me is the missed opportunities that come from not speaking out by using their own voices; instead I find them hiding behind an email.

If I ask someone to schedule a meeting and they are having trouble reaching the contact by email, I'm always reminding them: "Please pick up the phone to schedule this meeting." And I'm not just saying it to nag. These opportunities to speak live are great practice to use your voice and modulate it in a way that gives you confidence. It's important to feel good and self-assured as you learn to get your point across in the workplace.

Technology makes you think that if you've done something like send an email, you've made contact in the same way you do in real life. But what if nobody reads or acts on that email? You've missed an opportunity to relate, and just talk to people around you. And that creates missed opportunities in your career.

Look Up from Your Phone

Young women who are able to make eye contact, harness their focus, and look confident in what they are saying and how they are saying it with their words and body language, are truly memorable.

They stand out in a time when social media and technology are rapidly gaining influence over our lives. When you truly connect with someone on a human level, you make a strong impression, which can really make a difference in your professional relationships. Whether you're a millennial or not, you are likely part of this staggering statistic: the average person looks at their phone approximately forty-seven times a day, according to Deloitte's 2017 Global Mobile Consumer Survey.

Phone addiction is something that affects everyone, including me. I would be a total hypocrite to say, "Get off your phone!" because the truth is, I'm on my phone all the time.

The reality is that it's affecting young people more because you're facing a lifetime of phone dependency—your generation already has a deep connection with and need to be on your phones. You even feel a sense of anxiety when your phones are out of sight. Young adults 18 to 24 are more phone-dependent than any other age group, reportedly checking their phones *eighty-six* times a day, according to the same study. Millennials and the generations that follow are being hit the hardest.

What I can say from personal experience is that a phone dependency affects how people view you at work. It affects your demeanor and your professional persona. I've seen it time and time again.

I'll be honest: it makes me nervous dealing with young professionals who are constantly on their phones. I cringe when I ask an assistant to write an important fact or give him or her directions for a task, and then watch them whip out their iPhone to type down my notes. I beg them to carry a notepad! To write it all down physically.

Carrying a notepad is not just for show. It demonstrates professionalism, and most important, your notes are tangible. I'm always wondering, "Where is it going when they put it in their phone?" You're typing away work notes on your iPhone and suddenly your significant other texts you; you get a call; your battery dies; and so on. Then you look up at your boss and say, "Um, can you repeat that?" after she's just spent five minutes going over directions on a task. Save yourself (and your bosses!) and write it down.

There are any number of ways a phone can be distracting to those around you. Typing your supervisor's notes on your phone, taking calls or texts during meetings, getting stuck texting at your desk: all of it detracts from your professionalism, and makes it seem that you're not fully engaged.

Yes, there may be times when you need to handle time-sensitive information quickly on the phone. But the real reason I want people to use pen and paper is because you can look up and make eye contact and really connect. It's harder to do that with a phone. So take that screen away when you really want to engage with someone. Turn it upside down.

For young professionals just entering the workforce, putting the phone down not only makes you appear more attentive and professional, it does good things for our brains. It actually helps us think better.

Nicholas Carr, author of *The Shallows: What the Internet Is Doing to Our Brains*, lays out what's really happening beneath the surface: "What's interesting and concerning is that more recent research shows that just having a phone around, even it's not notifying or alerting you, even if you're not using it, seems to make us less capable of doing high-level thinking."

It undercuts your cognitive performance and ability to finish other tasks. Carr adds: "Results from two experiments indicate that even when people are successful at maintaining sustained attention—as when avoiding the temptation to check their phones—the mere presence of these devices reduces available cognitive capacity. Moreover, these cognitive costs are highest for those highest in smartphone dependence."

Researchers at the University of Chicago have dubbed this the "brain-drain hypothesis."

Carr confirms that "Our minds have limited cognitive ability to apply to any task. Some of that cognitive capacity is, in essence, being hijacked by your phone." In other words, part of your brain is monitoring and thinking about your phone. That leaves fewer resources to do other things.

If you are starting out in the workplace, you've got to be extra wary of distractions that keep your eye off the ball. If you're prone to frequently scrolling through social media, Carr's insight might be especially troubling. Finding yourself at your desk with your phone out even if you're not using it can get your mind thinking about all the things you could be doing with it—Facebook, Instagram, Twitter, or whatever other apps you spend your time on. Especially now that our social lives are so wrapped up in our phones.

It's going to make you fidgety and less likely to concentrate on work you need to get done!

Having a phone nearby "pulls some of your cognitive resources away from whatever you're trying to do, because you're thinking about your phone and what might be going on there," Carr adds.

Cal Newport refers to something called the "social media residue effect," the impact of switching your attention and reducing your cognitive abilities.

He explains: "If you're working and you glance at your phone, now we know that context switch comes at a real cost. It really takes a while for your cognitive capacity to return (to the task at hand). This is why having social media on your phone is so dangerous, because these apps have been engineered with billions of dollars to make you want to look at them."

Newport goes as far as to say, "Tech conglomerates are spending massive amounts of money to keep you looking at your phone as much as possible.

"It's important to keep in mind at this point that Facebook's market cap is almost twice as high as ExxonMobil's. It's almost twice as much money in extracting your attention as it is extracting oil out of the ground."

They've got to make their money somehow! But it comes at a cost to you if you have trouble managing time offline. In other words, if you're trying to focus on a task at hand, and you're doing a quick smartphone check every ten minutes or so, "you are putting yourself in a persistent state of reduced capacity," says Newport.

"A researcher at Stanford said that if you are constantly doing these attention switches…even if you are away from these distractions, your mind is unable to focus as well. You are permanently rewiring your brain to have a hard time sustaining concentration, even in the absence of distraction."

Newport observes that if you are in a job that's considered knowledge work, where your attention and ability to concentrate are required to do your job well, and you are constantly on your phone, "It's like being a professional athlete who smokes. It's an activity that you are doing in your personal life that is directly making you worse at what you are doing for a living."

Smartphones and tablets, along with social media applications like Twitter, have adapted to a generation that demands quick and digestible ways to understand the world around us. As a result, we're more and more comfortable with the short text, the recap, the summary.

Like all of us, my friend Martha Stewart sees the change in the way people are getting their information and how it is affecting the workplace. The newest members of the workforce are used to scanning through everything—through headlines, Instagram, apps. You are constantly shifting your brains to the next thing that catches your attention. But then, how do you develop your ability to contextualize and read between the lines?

Martha says "It's easy for people to get in the habit of reading synopses and reading headlines, and not get down to the nitty-gritty."

Martha worries that young professionals "know what a celebrity wore or said on the red carpet last night—but all that's from headlines. That's Instagram, a photograph…and when you want to tell them to go plant an apple tree, they don't know how. They don't know how big the hole has to be and how to dig it. My business is all about teaching, and in order to teach, you have to do the research, talk to the experts, and put information into context for the reader."

You might not care about planting an apple tree—or creating a business plan! But here is the bottom line: being super-technology-dependent can weaken your ability to think critically when a solution is not immediately in front of you.

That's not to say that you can't figure out how to do things on your own, since everything can be researched now with a simple Google search; but as Martha Stewart says: "You have to go further than a Google search, a skim of Wikipedia, or a bottom-line review. Develop curiosity. Challenge yourself to really delve into subject matter with profundity. Limit the surface information you take in so that you can allow room for deeper information. These are habits I encourage in my workforce."

According to studies, Martha is onto something. Nicholas Carr points out that skimming can be an important way of gathering information: "Sometimes we want to just scan the information environment and find what's interesting. That's an important skill to have."

TheSkimm newsletter, for example (whose amazing young founders are highlighted in this book!), is a great tool to start the day by scanning important news headlines from around the world. Sometimes you don't have time to read everything in depth.

The challenge is to hold yourself accountable once in a while and turn off the flow of information. If you are always relying on scanning, it hinders your ability to think deeply and conceptually.

Carr explains, "If you're always scanning, you're getting little pieces of information, but never connecting them to the bigger picture."

The big danger, he says, is that "we're training ourselves, thanks to the technology, to always be in skim/scan mode and never turn that off and get into deeply attentive mode, through which we make these mental associations that really enrich our thoughts and give us big-picture conceptualization."

It turns out that if you are constantly training your brain to graze over the highlights, it affects your ability to do your job, and might impact the way you approach your career, your goals, and your relationships.

As a business mogul, Martha Stewart notes how technology has affected her own life. She got her first computer in 1982. When she discovered search engine optimization, she told herself: "Wow, this is fantastic, now I can save so much time, I don't have to go to the library.

"But you know what? It was good to go to the library. It was good to have to open books and read some chapters before you get down to the facts you need. Now the facts are all there, but they're not curated the way we should be curating. The Internet

100

has not been the great time-saver we wanted it to be. In fact, it's eaten up all of our time."

For André Leon Talley, some of the young people who've worked for him appear to lack a thorough understanding of what it takes to complete a complex task.

"It's all on their computers, it's not in their heads," he tells me.

Psychologists have dubbed this reaction the "Google effect": the idea that if we take for granted the fact that we can look up a fact or figure on a search engine, we are less likely to give it mental effort. This is based on a 2011 study led by Columbia University's Betsy Sparrow and Harvard memory expert Daniel Wegner. The information we decide to encode in our heads gives way to critical and conceptual thinking. If we rely more and more on smartphones for answers, we'll have less context to build off ideas, and solutions to problems.

Nicholas Carr wrote in the *Wall Street Journal*, "Only by encoding information in our biological memory can we weave the rich intellectual associations that form the essence of personal knowledge and give rise to critical and conceptual thinking. No matter how much information swirls around us, the less stocked our memory, the less we have to think with."

Another study, published in a 2013 *Scientific American* article, suggests that the more you rely on your smartphone and Google searching skills to find answers and solutions, the sooner you'll end up suffering from "delusions of intelligence."

Nicholas Carr underscores the need for hard-won smarts: "What people need to understand is what makes you valuable as an employee, in many cases, is that you can take on really hard challenges and get them done, and get them done efficiently and well."

Building Emotional Fluency

Joanna Coles makes an important observation about the millennials she has worked with and managed: "I see a lot of millennials who are unable to get up and talk to someone, who are unable to have a conversation. And those are the skill sets that in the end will deliver. Anybody can send an email, anybody can post, but not everyone can make a call or have a meeting and get someone to change their mind.

"Those are the skill sets that I think we need more of, and I'm not seeing an enormous quantity. I think that we are dealing with a generation who find dealing with people in the moment difficult and have an ability to retreat into a digital world and think that sending an email or text or posting is enough. It's not. And it's very hard to stand out in the digital world because it's so crowded. I think the skill set that I am impressed by the most is the live skill set, the skill set of real conversation and real emotional connection. I think it is missing in the workforce."

> Anybody can send an email, anybody can post, but not everyone can make a call or have a meeting and get someone to change their mind.
> —JOANNA COLES

She tells me the story of her former assistant at *Cosmopolitan,* who was having trouble creating fluency, for the simple reason that he was hiding behind his email instead of getting out there and using his voice.

It was his job to help get ahold of managers and talent in the entertainment industry on Joanna's behalf. But somehow, he was never comfortable speaking to people over the phone. He constantly hid behind his email waiting for answers.

Joanna describes him: "He is a super-smart kid. He moved from his native Russia to Italy and picked up Italian within three months; then his family moved to America. He landed in Brooklyn and taught himself how to speak English by watching episodes of *I Love Lucy* and *Seinfeld.* Eventually he came to my office having worked in the music business. Super-smart guy, but just was not used to picking up the phone and calling people."

And every day Joanna would find herself telling him, "You need to call them, you need to call them. Why haven't you called them?" As a result, the assistant was constantly missing opportunities to connect and build a network for himself instead of being head-down in his administrative tasks.

The reality is that it takes more work to find other ways to get ahold of someone other than email. Joanna adds: "It takes a bit of effort to find someone's phone number. You can usually guess someone's email, but you can't guess someone's phone number."

Once this young man got on the phone, his career accelerated in a big way.

Joanna tells me: "He started to realize that people responded to him—and they loved him. He started going out on meetings. Now, literally, some of the top artists in the world call him, and perform for him one-on-one in studios because they want his feedback on their new songs and their new albums.

"He's gone from being someone who didn't even speak English at the age of thirteen to becoming unbelievably fluent in the language, and then emotionally fluent."

Joanna's former assistant went on to run music partnerships and talent booking for all magazines at Hearst before leaving for an even bigger opportunity.

And in her experience, this has happened repeatedly with entry-level assistants and associates she's worked with. When they do pick up the phone and start calling, they find themselves being much more effective, efficient, and more comfortable communicating.

It's a learned practice, but for some reason it's a bit more work for your generation. Joanna tells me that when young employees realize that, they say, "I can't believe I didn't call earlier."

Joanna adds: "There is no substitute for picking up the phone or going to someone's office. Wait outside the door if you need to, but that is how you get stuff done. A phone call is always better than an email, unless it's some legal detail that you need a record of."

Cal Newport, author of *Deep Work* and associate professor at Georgetown University, has studied social media and its effect on millennials. Cal points to research from Sherry Turkle at the Massachusetts Institute of Technology, who has done a lot of anthropological case studies of young people in office settings.

Her research shows how uncomfortable young people have become with face-to-face conversation.

You saw how the small changes put into practice by Joanna Coles's assistant at *Cosmopolitan* really helped move him along professionally. And it was all because he decided to connect with people outside of a computer screen! He used his voice to engage and communicate in real time.

Cal says that the lack of face-to-face communication is causing real problems in the workplace: "There's a hugely rich stream of information that comes from sitting down and talking with someone. We're wired and evolved for it; it's the key to successful communication. But if you're uncomfortable with it, if you are only comfortable communicating via short text messages and emails, you miss all that rich information stream. It causes lots of issues in the workplace, all sorts of misunderstandings and unnecessary resentments."

Those information streams Cal points to are really missed opportunities that, in some cases, could sideline your career.

Think about the pitch Daniela gave me on the plane that day that jump-started the second phase of her career. She came to me with her idea about access for young women of underrepresented backgrounds and spoke with intensity. She was focused—which is something that I liked about her from the moment I met her five years ago.

She was so intent on making sure her thoughts and words were understood and resonating with me. That same day I made a speech in front of 500 people. I started that morning doing the three live hours of *Morning Joe* in one state and was in another by midafternoon. I was whisked to a cocktail party in the evening, where I chatted up elected officials in attendance, as well as women from the audience who stopped by to say hello. I was literally meeting and talking to hundreds of people throughout that day.

But the only thing I remember clearly from that day was the conversation I had with Daniela on the plane, because we connected on a human level about a shared interest. The moments that will get you where you want to go in life are those human interactions, those moments of clear communication, and the imprint you leave on people. And those are the types of moments we need to focus on more. They make a big difference in your career.

Social Fluency

Being socially fluent means being able to talk about various subjects with people at every level and be confident while doing it. You can set yourself apart early on by displaying a sense of maturity and ease in social situations. It's an incredibly important skill to have.

How do you establish rapport with colleagues at other levels, let alone connect with CEOs, directors, and partners? Start by finding moments to build rapport in different settings at work—even in subtle ways, such as taking advantage of a lull in a conference call with someone you might be working with on a project, notes Carla Harris, vice chairman and managing director at Morgan Stanley and author of *Strategize to Win: The New Way to Start Out, Step Up, or Start Over in Your Career.* Harris says to take advantage of those moments to build that relationship: "Ask them how long they've been doing this, what other kind of analysis have they done that looks like this? How did you end up in this business or role?"

You can ask these types of questions of anyone you work with in your office; it gives them an opportunity to ask and learn a little more about you as well.

Social fluency involves give and take. Be mindful that you're not talking someone's ear off, of course! But take opportunities to really learn and practice your conversational skills. These are the ways you are going to prove your maturity, your ability to project confidence, and your understanding of the nuances of an environment, because you are in tune with the people around you.

Joanna tells me about a friend of hers who is a great example of this type of social fluency: "She was always able to hold court, to have everybody in the room—no matter who they were—listen to her. I realized it was because she always had an unbelievable stock of stories. On any subject she had an interesting anecdote. And she could always make something relevant because she read and read and read." Her friend is not only an interesting person; she's alert to what interests her audience.

Being able to hold your own in conversation and relate to the people around you also calls for another element of effective communication: active listening.

Former White House director of communications for President George W. Bush, political analyst, novelist, and host of

MSNBC's *Deadline: White House* Nicolle Wallace has made a living curating the proper way to deliver and receive a message. Not only that, but working under President Bush, she mastered the art of effective communication.

Your first jobs are great opportunities to practice active listening, the kind that requires you to do so with your whole body. This type of listening can induce a natural reaction: "Sometimes the listening is so intense that you jump in, because you know exactly what the other person is saying. Listening doesn't necessarily mean sitting there silently. It means really hearing somebody. Sometimes I think people just listen and still don't hear."

One of the precursors to learning to really listen is a willingness to abandon everything that you thought you were going to say.

Nicolle knows what makes a great, a good, and a not-so-good, communicator. Having good interpersonal skills means being flexible: "I think that if you are really in tune with how the mood is changing or shifting or improving or worsening, you're flexible enough to maybe take a different position or make a different argument or introduce different facts.

"From that, you build an ability to react and be spontaneous and empathetic."

That spontaneity that Nicolle points to is so important when you're building your communication skills.

My associate Daniela explains it this way: "I see young people who are starting out and thinking too far ahead of what they're saying. When they're talking to you, it feels like they're not actually have a conversation, because they're thinking about the next thing that they're going to say.

"But having been there myself, I know that it's just nerves. You want to make sure that the conversation is flowing well, that there aren't any pauses. In some ways it's just our anxiety showing through."

Nicolle Wallace grew up in a household of four kids, and she felt the push and pull, the tension that comes from everyone trying to get a word in. During her time in the White House she observed a lot more people trying to get in their two cents and wanting to be seen as influential. She realized that her ability to listen and observe was just as important—if not more so—than her ability to speak well.

According to Nicolle, you look for windows of opportunity to show you are really listening, because good listeners are better communicators. You can do that by observing something that other people missed and by listening more intently: "In terms of picking up the emotional dynamics, in a room or in a workplace, there is just nothing more powerful than being the person that was listening the most intently and just watching the way someone talked. And I can catch myself saying to someone, 'What did you think and not say?'"

> ...there is just nothing more powerful than being the person that was listening the most intently and just watching the way someone talked.
> —NICOLLE WALLACE

Nicolle's study of the way people spoke allowed her to really flourish as the communications director for President Bush. She also found power in not always being the loudest, but by listening and then reacting to the issues at hand with a greater understanding of the problem—and then communicating a solution or message effectively.

When she started working for the Bushes, first Jeb and then George W., there was no texting, no reading between the Internet lines. It was face to face, so there was a much better chance to learn to read people and then engage in a reactive way. The challenge for millennials and Gen Z is that so much of their communication is on the phone or in texts, where there is no eye contact: "There's no reading a person's face. That is the challenge for your generation."

Josh Earnest has a few words of advice for young people on speaking out in a room: "Know what you're talking about. And don't be afraid to listen."

He tells me, "It's good to be energetic and to be engaged and eager to make a contribution—not to hesitate to hold up your hand and speak your mind. That needs to be tempered by some self-awareness, particularly for someone who's young, who's early in their career. Remember that you're still new to this, and that it's not a sign of weakness to listen.

"Don't be the first one to speak up; it's not an indication that you haven't done your homework, or that you're not smart, or that you don't have something to offer. And be judicious about knowing when to speak up, which is really important for a young person. Because I think a lot of young people think to themselves, 'I need to quickly show and prove my value,' which isn't a bad instinct, but you have other ways of showing your value than offering your opinion."

I agree with Josh. I understand the need to feel heard and raise your hand to offer a solution or problem when you are in a meeting. It's a natural reaction to feel like you want to contribute. But don't just blurt out something if you don't have real value to offer.

In these situations where you don't know what to say and want to avoid revealing any ignorance, just be still. Be still in a meeting. Be still in a moment when you feel like you should be doing something. If you have nothing to say, don't say it. You don't always have to say or do something amazing to bring attention to yourself. In fact, you could be doing something utterly boring really well and still stand out beautifully.

Young women in particular have to learn to point out what they do really well. But standing out awkwardly or making a point just to make a point, or asking a question just to ask a question, takes away from the real value of your professional persona. Better to do a really good job and pick your moments.

Earnest adds: "This instinct to weigh in needs to be tempered by awareness that there's more that you can learn. Sitting and listening, and not interjecting every time a thought comes to mind, isn't an indication that you're not engaged; people aren't going to think you aren't thinking about anything. Waiting until you are sure you know what you think, and until you're sure you have all the information needed to arrive at a conclusion before speaking up, is a valuable thing for people to keep in mind."

Each situation is of course different, and there are situations in which it's more appropriate to lean in and actively engage rather than sit back and listen. In creative environments, for instance, where you are expected to partake in brainstorming sessions, you might try a different approach.

Laura Brown of *InStyle* finds that in these team meetings, it's actually better to speak up: "If it's a pitch meeting, I'd rather people speak up with a bad idea than just sit there, because I forget the people that just sit there."

Creative brainstorming sessions are meant to generate possibilities, and somebody's half-baked idea may help someone else come up with an inspired one. Working for an advertising team is a different environment than, say, working for a politician or in news. Understanding your environment is key to effectively communicating in it.

It's crucial to observe the environment around you because that's how you pick up cues of what's welcomed and not welcomed. Follow the lead of your team members, and when you understand the dynamics of an office you'll know what kind of input is truly valued.

Communicating Effectively with Body Language

Body language plays a big role in effectively getting your message across. Just as your words matter in the workplace, so does your body language. It shows you are engaged and aware of the environment around you.

Even if you work in an office and sit in a cubicle, you should look physically open. This is what I mean: you're sitting at your desk, hunched over, scrolling through your Instagram feed. Sound familiar? I've certainly seen it.

Body language plays a big role in effectively getting your message across.

When you're just starting out in the workforce, you can't afford to look closed-down to your boss and colleagues. You should be able to make eye contact and connect with everything that's going on in the room: being on your phone is not going to help you do that.

In an office environment, you may not need to talk all the time—or even at all. But when you're engaged with a manager or a coworker in a conversation, you need to be taking it all in, asking questions, watching, and listening.

And it's hard when you're shy, especially for a woman. You might want to sort of disappear and sit at your desk and just do your job. You might think, "Okay, I'm doing my job, so someone's going to notice."

1. No one is going to notice.
2. You want to feel part of the room. You need to be physically open to do so.

Even if you're starting out and getting coffee, don't miss small ways to engage. Who are you bringing coffee to, what is their role, and how else can you be of service? When they say, "Thank you!" you can say, "You're welcome. Is there anything else you need?" Follow up. Be present and in the moment.

Start with Your Manager

A key opportunity for advancement starts with your ability to communicate effectively with your boss, or your direct report if you are in an industry that has one. Your boss is your most important colleague when you're starting out, and it's important to determine which communication style works best.

Carla Harris of Morgan Stanley thinks that being effective as you navigate your early career requires you to observe and get a read on your manager's behavior, and then really invest in understanding how he or she likes to communicate.

You should ask your manager how they prefer to communicate. Should you to stop by their office if you need clarification on something, or do they prefer email, instant message, or a phone call?

Another important element to help understand your manager's communication style is feedback. Harris says that you should be doing your part by asking for feedback directly.

Here is something important for young women to know when it comes to feedback: just because you are not getting real-time feedback all the time does not mean you're doing something wrong. Your boss has a million things to do and think about.

He or she might not have time to give you frequent real-time feedback. So before stressing out and doubting yourself, or wondering if you did something wrong (as women, this is often our first thought!), just ask and follow up!

Carla Harris suggests: "Say, 'Here's something I think I did well, and here's something I could have done a little better. Any thoughts about how we might have done this differently?'

Understand that if you don't get feedback every time, it's not because you did a bad job. If you've done a bad job, trust that they're going to say something. So in the space of silence, assume that's good." Above all, learn not to personalize situations at work too often. We women tend to do this. Feedback is good, but don't A) feel that you can't ask for it if you need it, or B) assume that your boss isn't happy with your work. Everyone is worried about their own performance; it's really helpful to assert yourself and to ask your boss questions about your progress if you need to!

> **Feedback is good, but don't A) feel that you can't ask for it if you need it, or B) assume that your boss isn't happy with your work.**

Build Your Value

Right off the bat, you've got to lay the foundation right. You've got to find ways to BUILD your value.

These building-block years are key to help shape and establish your value in the workplace: who you are as a professional and how you want to be known. It's an opportunity to soak everything in, learn as much as you can about your environment and the people around you, and perform tasks that come your way with deliberate focus. It's a time to find your bearings, perhaps make some mistakes, correct those mistakes, figure yourself out, and realize what you bring to the table—so that when the time comes for the next step you can clearly advocate for yourself. You can communicate your value because you have already worked at it—you won't have a shadow of a doubt what that value is!

CHAPTER SIX

EMBRACE YOUR ADVOCATING POWER

When you've gotten the hang of that first job, when you've paid your dues and made some meaningful contributions, you will finally have some leverage. Now's the time to learn how to advocate for yourself effectively—in every sense.

Whether you're lobbying for projects you want to take on, asking for a raise, or simply standing up for yourself when something doesn't sit well with you, you need to find your voice. Using your voice to ask for the things you want in the workplace is so important—and yes, money is often the reward!

It's common knowledge that women are less likely than men to make demands at work. Women value being liked; sometimes to our detriment. We go out of our way to make people comfortable, to adapt to fit the environment we're in, to make others feel at ease. We're less likely to speak up in a meeting, and more likely to meet later with other women to talk about what we really wanted to say.

Doing this day after day in the workplace will backfire in the long run—our impulse to be accommodating doesn't work at the negotiating table. Using language like "I'm sorry, I know this might be a bad time…" or "I don't want to be a problem, but…"

doesn't typically make a boss snap to attention and race to get you what you need.

...our impulse to be accommodating doesn't work at the negotiating table.

Literally the worst thing we can do is undermine ourselves by trying so hard to set a friendly tone and to avoid making the other person feel uncomfortable.

Men are less likely to have a problem with this. They don't think twice about speaking their mind and taking action to get what they want. This was one of the things I found true through my own experience with getting paid what I was worth when I first started at *Morning Joe*: that story inspired my first book. All the men around me were incredibly self-possessed, which really helped their negotiating power—not just when they were asking for more money, but whenever they wanted to push their ideas at work.

Young women, we found, consider it more intimidating to advocate for themselves in workplaces that are male-dominated. One young woman in her late 20s who worked in finance told us how proud she was of the work she had done. She had done everything her boss asked and gone above and beyond her role. Yet this thinking held her back from advocating for herself: "If I'm doing a good job, it's only a matter of time my job will get noticed."

That's only partly true. Good work rarely goes unnoticed. But to cash that in for your next step, you've got to find your voice. And not advocating for yourself effectively will leave you in the dust. In the past chapter we talked about being okay with taking the early months to absorb and listen. When you have done the work and have gone beyond your job description to move the needle at your company, it's important to recognize it and be able to articulate it.

Here's your call to action: *No one is going to do it for you.* If you've got the data, if you've got the proof of purchase of your value and your work has spoken for itself, what is really holding you back from speaking out at work? Every day you need to find a way to do it.

Here's your call to action: *No one is going to do it for you.*

I don't care if it's with the janitor, with a colleague, a manager, or the CEO. Every opportunity you have, you need to put yourself forward and find the words. Say you find yourself in the elevator with the CEO: You can say something like, "Hi, my name is so-and-so, I've been working on this project and the deal with XYZ, and boy, would I love to meet and show you what I've done."

And then GO. Open the door for yourself. Take what's frustrating you and making you feel negative and turn it into a positive. Use your voice. Find the words.

You may, of course, fail. But you're never going to get better unless you walk through that door and speak up for yourself. Nobody is going to do it for you; if you are trying the back door and talking to everyone except the person in the decision-making seat, hoping colleagues in the office will say something to advocate on your behalf, good luck! You'll be in the same job, if you're lucky, for many years, but you probably won't move up. That's just not how it works anymore.

It's time to step up and into your advocating power.

Young Women and Ambition

One of the challenges with finding the confidence to advocate for yourself is the self-consciousness around the word "ambition." There is a clear double standard: ambition in young men is a positive attribute, but in women? Not so much.

Research shows that both men and women react badly to young women who draw attention to themselves at work and are openly aggressive about their goals.

Joanna Coles worked with plenty of ambitious young women who wanted to get ahead in their careers. We spoke about the subject of ambition and the risk young women feel, in possibly turning people off by showing too much of it.

"One of the struggles for millennials who are ambitious is, how do they present that ambition in the world? If you present it too forcefully, without too much experience, you can put people off. And that's not because you're trying to appear ambitious, it's because they know that you haven't quite done the work to get where you want to be.

"People can sniff out fakes. Of course, we know that you should fake it until you make it, and that a lot of work is the art of confidence. But you must back it up with the work," Joanna tells me.

Overall, 69 percent of men and the same number of women see ambition in the workplace as a favorable attribute. However, there are some important differences among women based on race and ethnicity. Young Hispanic women are far less likely than white and black women to believe that being ambitious in the workplace is "mostly positive." Less than half (46 percent) of Hispanic women say that being ambitious in the workplace is "mostly positive," compared to 77 percent of whites and 75 percent of African Americans. The word "determined" does not carry the same baggage; there are no statistical differences by race.

The challenge is to be self-possessed and self-aware enough to ask for what you want only after you have built a foundation of work to reference. This isn't to say that you shouldn't speak up for yourself in the meantime: that's the core of my message! But you'll be most effective asking for more opportunity or more money when you have quantifiable results already on your balance sheet.

As the creative director of her own fashion and accessories company, Rebecca Minkoff has about 80 employees. Ninety percent of them are millennial! With this generation she sees a shift in how they approach ambition. She's noticed a change in attitude in that these young women are ready to step up for assignments they truly can make their own, while also supporting the greater good of the brand and team.

For this reason, she's worked hard on making her brand one that will "showcase the multidimensional, multifaceted beauty of women." Her brand manifesto embraces and celebrates all of the parts of being a woman: "When we embrace and celebrate our all, we believe anything can happen."

So how do you bring your whole self to work unapologetically while also being ambitious and learning to navigate your environment at work effectively? You work on the delivery and you focus on seizing opportunities.

Rebecca has this advice for finding that balance and debunking the entitlement rep: "I think that there's a fire in one's eye, a professionalism that still should be there. The millennial women that rise to the top in my company still display all the qualities of an entrepreneur, even if they're working for me. What they do well is take and seize opportunities, they go outside of their comfort zone, they push themselves, and they say yes to things that maybe make them uncomfortable, but discover that having taken a challenge, they can do that. That's what I look for now in hiring: someone that's not above anything, who takes every action you give them and does it with a lot of pride."

> The millennial women that rise to the top in my company still display all the qualities of an entrepreneur, even if they're working for me.
> —REBECCA MINKOFF

Fashion designer Tory Burch is taking steps to encourage ambition in young women.

Through the Tory Burch Foundation, she has launched a global #EmbraceAmbition initiative to empower women and girls to own their power and drive to achieve their goals, whether they are professional pursuits or are outside of the workplace.

Tory first started thinking about the double standard for women during an interview with the *New York Times* in 2014. The reporter asked if she was ambitious, and she found herself brushing off the question, saying that the word annoyed her. After the interview, the feedback she heard was: "Why are you not owning your ambition?"

Tory thought to herself, "Of course, I was then, and I am now, ambitious." But it was a clarifying moment for her. She realized that she was feeling a stigma that all women feel: that somehow it was better not to show ambition, for fear that it would be considered unattractive. She realized a man probably wouldn't have been asked that question—simply because of his gender. From that moment on, she decided to encourage women to own it.

Tory, whose staff is two-thirds millennials, believes the young professionals who are really getting it right find the balance between pursuing their own goals and embracing being part of the team: "Taking ownership in what you're doing is something we're working on with the whole team. Being collaborative is something I think is essential: not always taking credit, but really sharing credit with those around you."

Though owning your ambition is a good thing, taking credit for everything can be seen as too "me-centric." After all, when you are starting out, much of your success is thanks to a group effort.

Jane Park, founder of Julep Beauty, had a similar experience learning to think from a team perspective in her early years as a business consultant. "I think it's important to look outside of yourself and realize that it's a group journey. What's your role in what the whole company is doing, no matter how big the company is?"

Park stresses the need to make yourself valuable by thinking about how you can benefit the team you work with: "What is your team trying to accomplish at Starbucks, for example, and what can you do to make your team more likely to be successful? A specific piece of tactical advice I give people is that it's your job to make your bosses' lives easier, and not in a way that is invisible. How can you make a difference and make sure that the whole team is likely to be successful?

"Once you see the world that way, it's so different than seeing it as just about you, and whether you're getting an A or an A plus."

Park cites an epiphany she had after an important presentation: "As a junior consultant I had worked really hard on my part. I thought I did a really good job. As we were loading up on the plane, I asked my manager, 'How did you think that went?' Meaning, really, 'How do you think I did?'

"He launched into two big things: one was whether we were going to make a difference for the company we were working for. The second thing was how *he* did, because it was his major presentation in front of all these senior executives. It didn't occur to him at all that I was asking about me.

"As it turns out, you're the only one walking around thinking about you. Everybody else is thinking about themselves, or something else."

The lesson here is that you can be ambitious and still focus on the needs of the team. As women, we have to stop personalizing everything and just look at the big picture sometimes. When you are starting out, your ambition shows in the work you do— how you contribute to the group effort.

As you move along in your career, you're going to find that you may need to be more vocal about your ambitions. That's the time to point at everything you've done to move along team goals and company initiatives, or to improve the numbers in your division.

Know that being personally ambitious and looking out for the team's best interests are not mutually exclusive: in fact, they can reinforce each other.

Challenges

Women need to get used to championing themselves and telling others how great they are when the credit is due. Most of us hate doing that. But after you've had some success and have a track record that shows your value, it's time to start getting comfortable promoting yourself. Sometimes that means making the argument that you're the best person for the job: it means sticking your neck out. And even ambitious and assertive women have trouble with this.

One thing that gets in the way? The "imposter syndrome." Daniela admits that she struggled with this after finding some success in her career: "I would look around me and feel like I had somehow been 'allowed in' without necessarily feeling adequate or as smart as everyone else in the room."

Shifting your perspective by mentally listing your achievements can help boost your confidence. That's a key part of embracing your ambitious. Get over the fact that you are somehow lucky to be there. You've earned it! It's time to own it.

Shifting your perspective by mentally listing your achievements can help boost your confidence. That's a key part of embracing your ambition.

Daniela observes, "I had to force myself to constantly remember everything I had battled on my own and the things I had to overcome that got me here. In reality, I *did* have a seat at the table; I had earned it—but part of being confident enough to participate and be comfortable asserting yourself is giving yourself credit."

Jessica O. Matthews, founder and CEO of the renewable power company Uncharted Power, knows the biases in her field well enough to be empowered to debunk them. "As a woman and a person of color, I can almost always tell you that I don't match the stereotype of what you would think from someone who's a leader in STEM in their career."

Matthews has a list of accolades including *Fortune*'s Most Promising Women Entrepreneurs list. She garnered a spot on the *Forbes* 30 under 30 list and was named Harvard University

Scientist of the Year in 2012. She's managed to achieve tremendous success in a field that typically applies the word "innovator" to men only: "[The stereotype is a] man who looks a certain way, with a certain background—that's what we've been told it means to be an innovator."

The STEM field, she notes, has been known to include individuals who are not "particularly charismatic, who you don't expect to present, speak, or engage well." One of the challenges she encountered from early on was having to prove this stereotype wrong. "When people hear me speak about what we do, they assume that I'm a hired spokesperson and not the chief technical architect for our business.

"Often in STEM, because women are able to communicate, collaborate, and pull together teams and play chief psychology officer really well, people are going to try to push you into product management."

Jessica proves that women need to be more vigilant about their own path for advancement. You are your own best advocate!

To women working in STEM, she advises: "Don't shy away from leadership, or from taking technology projects that are people-oriented....Make sure you also find yourself in the lab sometimes, at least a little bit throughout the week. Make sure you're not totally removed from what's happening technically and make sure you're staying abreast of [the latest advancements] and keeping yourself sharp."

Matthews says that part of getting the big projects in her field requires being vocal about wanting those opportunities, but also "mentally preparing yourself that it is going to be an upward battle." There is power in knowing what you're up against, and what you bring to the organization.

She adds: "Every individual has a unique perspective based on their gender, their race, their ethnicity, their religion, their socioeconomic status. So coming forward is actually what allows us to create solutions and design technologies and systems for a broader society, and make the world a better place."

Barbara Corcoran, real estate tycoon, businesswoman, and investor on ABC's *Shark Tank,* knows how to speak up and ask for what she wants. "We (women) don't want to be rude, and people think asking about money is rude—too abrupt. And I too made many bad business deals [early in my career] because I felt like I couldn't address the money issue until I got older."

After some memorable deals in which she was vastly underpaid compared to male competitors, Barbara learned her lesson well. She now asks for what she deserves, and she's not apologetic. "I always negotiate back, but I land close to or above where I wanted. I've got that trick down." But learning to use her voice took time: "Even on *Shark Tank,* it took me two years to learn how to tell the guys to shut the f*** up when I was saying something, because my voice is smaller."

Her advice for young women is to never to forget the skills you bring to the table: "It's not that I was ever in a situation where I felt that I was worth less than the guy that I was trying to compete with.

"In fact, I would have to say, in every situation I frankly valued myself more, because I knew I would work harder than anyone else in the universe on whatever I was trying to accomplish, because I am that kind of person. And I doubted whether my competitor was cut from the same cloth.

"If you're going to work harder, and do a better job, then ask for more money than you think your male counterpart would. Women will pussy-foot around it. Just say, 'Here is why I think I am worth more: A, B, and C,'" she advises.

> Every minute you spend preparing gives you two minutes' worth of confidence—truly, every time—even if you never have to use what you prepare.
>
> —BARBARA CORCORAN

Barbara is able to ask for what she deserves because she's done her homework. She always comes to the negotiating table over-prepared. "I am a very good overpreparer because of my own insecurity. What you get from that is not only clarity as to how you are going to express yourself; you also gain great confidence because you spent the time preparing.

"Every minute you spend preparing gives you two minutes' worth of confidence—truly, every time—even if you never have to use what you prepare."

Confidence Factors

Confidence plays a big part in propelling women forward or holding them back. It's not always easy for women to catch their stride and feel like they've "got this." In the early phases of their careers, men typically start out with a confidence advantage.

Our polling in collaboration with Harvard Kennedy School's Institute of Politics found that young women were far less likely than men to feel prepared for finding their first professional job after graduation. As many as 7 in 10 indicated that they did not feel prepared, and this was especially true for women who graduated with social science and humanities degrees.

Once in the door, women are more confident that they will perform well, and the confidence gap with men wanes. Overall, the research shows that the majority of the unpreparedness comes before stepping in the door to the job you want.

Why does it take women a longer time to feel confident at the beginning of their careers?

Katty Kay has researched the truth about women and confidence extensively.

One of the biggest surprises she found was that she had assumed that women in their 20s today would be far more confident than women of earlier generations. She says, "We found that this was not the case. And in some ways, there are more pressures on younger women today than there were before. There are different pressures, but just as many as when we were their age."

The data shows that some of the confidence crisis is driven by social media. Katty observes: "The pressure to get 500 'likes' on your Facebook page or your Instagram or your Twitter feed exacerbates a feeling that you have to be able to do everything perfectly all the time."

Social media can be a great tool, but not if you allow it to affect your self-esteem and confidence. Being in the public eye, I'm scrutinized on air and online every day, and at this point I have a pretty thick skin. People post comments intended to make me feel bad about myself on a regular basis—including none other than the President of the United States, Donald J. Trump. Trump likes to call me "low I.Q. Crazy Mika," and memorably—and falsely—proclaimed to the world he saw me "bleeding badly from a face-lift" at a New Year's Eve party.

The hate tweets that followed were like nothing I'd ever experienced before. The Internet can be a ruthless place, but I can handle that. It's part of being in the public eye.

Yet I wonder if the same can be said for young women starting out. I discussed this with my coauthor, Daniela; she agrees that millennials inevitably feel a deep sense of vulnerability about how their online selves are being perceived. Counting "likes" and the need to make your photos perfectly filtered alters your state of reality. Too much energy goes into it, which inevitably damages your true sense of worth.

Insights from the Harvard-led focus groups corroborate this, showing that there is a growing sense of anxiety stemming from a combination of social media (curating for an audience that might not reflect your true self) and the unknowns of leaving a college community and entering the workplace. *Nervous, murky, uncertain,* and *anxious* are all adjectives that were used in the focus groups conducted.

Growing Your Confidence

Katty Kay writes about two types of confidence: the kind that is acquired superficially through validation and compliments, and the kind that comes from achievements.

As Katty describes it: "The confidence that we get from outside sources, from 'likes' on Facebook or the fact that fifteen people just followed you on Instagram or from our professor telling us we did a good job or a boss raving about you or a critic writing a good review if you're a musician, for example: that's volatile confidence. It's volatile because it can be taken away again very quickly; you can lose it very fast. And it is not a reliable form of confidence. It is very ephemeral and fragile—it's like crack; you're never gonna have enough of it."

Katty's advice is to build true confidence by finding opportunities for personal growth, "where you actually build something, where you master a problem, or you overcome a hurdle." These successes, however small, create a tangible sense of confidence that no selfie post with seventy-plus likes can compare to: it's lasting, it's real, and it stores itself in your brain.

According to Katty, what builds real confidence are things like learning to swim or some other new physical endeavor; putting in effort when the going gets hard; teaching yourself another language; pushing yourself to run for a leadership position and going out and getting the necessary votes. All these things are difficult, and can change the way you view yourself, because you have put yourself out there and learned to trust your ability to meet new challenges.

That's the kind of confidence you can put in the bank.

Katty began building her own confidence through solid and empowering achievements, moments that helped bolster her even when she felt uncomfortable. And if you look at Katty, you'd never guess that she was ever self-conscious. She's extremely smart, graduated from a top university, is multilingual, and has impressive journalism acumen. Yet there was a time when she wondered if she was capable of even raising her hand in a room full of other journalists.

"I remember when I was young, the thing I used to find very hard was going to press conferences and asking questions. The idea that the whole room would turn around and look at me, and then I'd blush and stumble, and I'd probably sweat. And everybody would think, 'Oh, my God, how could she ask such a stupid question? She doesn't know what she's talking about.'"

Katty worked on her confidence by pushing herself out of her comfort zone: "I would literally force myself to put my hand up and get a question out, and by doing that, I probably did blush. And it might not have been the most intelligent question in the history of questions.

"I may have stumbled over the words a bit, but I'd gotten through it, and the sky didn't fall on my head and the earth didn't swallow me whole. I was still there. And with each subsequent interview or press conference or public engagement of that kind, I knew I'd survived the last one.

"I realize that some people reading this won't think that getting up and raising your hand in a room full of people is that hard, but that's irrelevant. It's about getting through hard or uncomfortable moments that you define as such: that's the only way to really build up confidence in a worthwhile way," Katty says.

She explains that the process of building true confidence is like building a wall, where every achievement, even a small one, acts like a physical building block.

> ...you learn confidence by absorbing rejection and moving on.
> —KATTY KAY

"I had banked a brick of confidence. Each time you do something that is hard for you and you get through it and you survive, you have another brick to put in your wall of confidence. And no one can take that away from you. For every single person there will be something else that's hard, but once you push through it and you overcome the obstacle, you realize that you can master a situation. That's very empowering—much more so than someone on your cell phone telling you you're great."

Katty told me another story with a key lesson: you learn confidence by absorbing rejection and moving on.

As an illustration, she told me about a literary agent she interviewed for her book *The Confidence Code*. The agent had both a young female and a young male associate. The female associate would make appointments to see her with prepared notes, but then would be terribly upset if the meeting didn't go as planned or if her ideas were rejected.

On the other hand, the male associate, who was much newer, would stop by her door casually every day and fling out ideas—every day. Katty reports: "Half the time it really annoyed her, and she'd have to back him down like an annoying puppy dog. But this young associate knew that, at some point, one of his ideas would stick, and he would rise, while the female associate wouldn't."

Considering this scenario, the agent's advice to young women is to try something called "fail fast," which involves throwing out ideas—even if half of them, or three-quarters of them—might be rejected: "But if you don't keep throwing them out, your chances of having one of them stick are diminished compared to your male counterparts, who are doing exactly that."

Don't hold yourself back or restrict yourself from pushing ideas out there! And if you have an idea that you put out there and it gets batted down, don't allow yourself to use that as an excuse not to put out the next one. Women are known to take things to heart, and have a more difficult time not taking failure personally. We need to work harder at this. It's important that you put yourself, and your ideas, out there. We're women, and we're at the table. We're no longer on the sidelines when it comes to our advocating power. We need to use that power and start talking. And it's not always easy.

Keeping Up Confidence

In her time at the global think tank Center for Talent Innovation (CTI), where she spent a decade researching women in STEM, Laura Sherbin found that those who embrace and keep up their confidence are, not surprisingly, much more likely to be successful. Through the interviews she's conducted, and the data on women in STEM that she's analyzed, she's found that success can be a tough slog.

"Women talk about really proactively feeding their confidence, knowing that there are going to be onslaughts, and that they have to keep building it up. They find they have to surround themselves with people who will help build it up for them."

Keeping up confidence is very difficult for women across all ethnicities, but interestingly, CTI data shows that among women who are hugely successful, black women and Latinas are often much more confident than their white and Asian counterparts.

> Women talk about really proactively feeding their confidence, knowing that there are going to be onslaughts, and that they have to keep building it up. They find they have to surround themselves with people who will help build it up for them.
> —LAURA SHERBIN

She points to an interview she had with a very senior African American technologist. When Laura asked where her confidence came from, the woman replied: "It's because I had to work so hard."

Perhaps because her confidence had been tested so often and so thoroughly, it had grown strong as steel.

"She felt that [her innate confidence] was this sorting mechanism—in some ways, I think that she felt it was the 'survival of the most confident,' if you will."

CTI found a similar relationship to confidence for many of the STEM professionals who were of Latina background. As Laura recalls, "They spoke of their family and community structure building up their confidence in the industry. And how for them to really get through all their obstacles, all of those around them were really building them up—and that made such a huge difference.

"One of the things I have always admired in a lot of the Hispanic or Latino employee resource groups is the ability of the group and the community that's created there to support each other—and I think that that might be one of the pieces that's influencing those higher levels of confidence. It's really something we can all learn from."

Women who have struggled from the beginning and learned to solve real problems have a confidence you can't break. My coauthor, Daniela, whose struggles you read about earlier, really found her voice and advocating power early on.

To quote Katty Kay, Daniela had strong "building blocks" of confidence.

As she describes it: "I've always had a 'fake it till you make it' mentality. When you grow up with few financial resources, little access to valuable work mentors, and no legal status, you have to make your own path. I always felt I had too much to lose if I *didn't* believe I could do it."

All her life, Daniela has had to capitalize on moments of confidence.

There was no time for that self-doubt.

Daniela was also smart enough to know not to ask for outside opinions. If anyone knew the battle ahead of her, they would have easily brought her down and given her a "reality check."

You gain confidence, as she did, by mastering a problem or finding a solution to a predicament. It positively changes the way you see yourself, and you build strength from the core outward—an asset that will benefit you continuously in the workplace.

Confidence, and the ability to act on that confidence, need to go together. Young women need to work hard to quiet those whispers of self-doubt. It's so hard for us! We all know we can be our own worst enemy. As you navigate your early and mid-career, you've got to be alert to those nagging doubts, and—like Katty Kay at those early press conferences—get out of your comfort zone and force yourself to speak up.

U.S. hockey Olympic gold medalists Monique Lamoureux-Morando and Jocelyne Lamoureux-Davidson built those confidence blocks early on, too.

Growing up, they both competed and played against boys in a variety of different sports. They were natural athletes, which gave them innate self-assurance. Jocelyne says, "We were normally two of the better athletes on boys' teams. At a young age we were confident that we could play against the boys. And we always had each other, which also gave us confidence."

Practicing and preparing, day after day, added essential reinforcement. "We're confident that we've done everything we can to be the best athletes we can be.... We moved away from home when we were 15 and went to a boarding school to pursue our hockey dreams." They still practice day in and day out, but as Jocelyne says, there's always "an element of the unknown: that you can work your entire life and not accomplish your goal."

Being okay with uncertainty and pushing through it is another confidence builder. Jocelyne tells me: "Knowing that you can only control what you can control and putting in the work—in athletics or in life—transfers to success. There are definitely heartbreaks and you don't always get the things you worked for. But you've certainly put your best foot forward to try and accomplish something great, something that's worth attaining."

Monique gives this example to reinforce the point: "In Sochi in 2014, we lost in the gold medal game 3 to 2 in overtime, and we were up 2 to nothing with about two minutes left in the game when Canada tied it up. We go into overtime, and we end up losing—one of the most heartbreaking losses we've ever experienced. And I think the biggest thing we've taken away from that is the amount our team learned and grew from that loss.

"It really forced us to look within ourselves and our team-mates, and figure out what we really needed to do to be better to make sure the outcome was going to be different the next time around. It's not easy to self-evaluate when you've had failure, but I think that's when you learn and grow the most. Winning can teach you something, but losing can teach you much more."

Get Used to Talking About Yourself

For women on television, projecting confidence, poise, and control would seem as natural as breathing. But even some of the best in the business—legends—and some of my role models in the world of journalism still have to think about how they present themselves.

Take Meredith Vieira, a veteran in network television and seasoned journalist. She exudes strength, warmth, and confidence. That is what she projects to the world—part of her professional brand.

One of the ways she so clearly communicates that message about herself to millions of viewers is through her voice: the tonality of it—the way she projects it. As someone who works in television and really understands the technical aspects of voice projection, I can say she has one of the best voices in the business. She has the lower register in her voice that conveys a sense of comfort and being at ease.

I spoke to Meredith about how she's able to appear so comfortable in her own skin. She told me it's something she practices every day.

Meredith makes a habit of saying mantras: "I literally say to myself, yes, I am an older woman, but with that comes maturity and experience and knowledge that I couldn't acquire any other way than by, every day, getting up and learning more."

She repeats this to herself constantly: "I think that if you project what you want to be, then people will see it, it'll be reflected back at you. I really believe that. It helps me."

...if you project what you want to be, then people will see it, it'll be reflected back at you.

—MEREDITH VIEIRA

Every day Meredith walks down a path in her neighborhood talking to herself, maybe looking a little crazy, but not caring. This really is a great way to practice boosting your confidence, to articulate what you stand for, and to practice communicating effectively.

Meredith tells me, "In order to feel empowered, you need to believe in yourself." Repeating her mantras, talking to herself, and giving herself pep talks has, and still does, work for her.

She adds: "The more that you do it, the stronger you get at it. And it's what's in you, your essence, that you're developing. It's always there in a rough form, and you're polishing it to such a great shine that it can really emerge. When you're really yourself, it's amazing how you project that, and how other people perceive it. If you're comfortable in your skin, it makes other people feel comfortable and confident about you."

Another practice Meredith finds helpful to work on being comfortable with yourself and clarifying your message to the world? Writing letters to yourself.

No matter your age, as Meredith told me, there is something especially clarifying in finding your voice in the middle of confusion. She told me about a trip she took to a retreat in California. She was feeling not-so-great about herself. She was confused, and at a turning point in her career. At the retreat, they instructed her to write a letter to herself.

A few months later, she received it in the mail. When her letter arrived, she assumed she'd forgotten to pay the last half of the bill; but what she found were her own thoughts about what she had hoped to get out of the retreat—where she hoped to be in her life and work in a few months. To her, the letter served as a token of clarity.

She encourages others to write letters about themselves, or in a journal, or wherever you are forced to think about yourself. The more you get used to talking about yourself, and what you want from a job or even a relationship, the more comfortable you get at being in your own skin. To vocalize or write that is powerful.

Getting comfortable talking about how great you are is something you have to constantly practice. It's an exercise I encourage all women, young and old, to do. PRACTICE, PRACTICE, PRACTICE! Because when your moment comes to advocate for yourself, you've got to find the words and know what it feels like to say them with confidence.

Speaking Out in Real Time and Knowing Your Red Lines

At the beginning of your career, there should be very few instances in which you are saying no to professional opportunities, but you should always be vocal when a situation crosses the line professionally.

Women need to know where their "red lines" are and be ready to use their voice the moment something doesn't feel right. Especially in the era of #MeToo, women are empowered to simply state, "I'm not okay with that" or "This makes me uncomfortable," and alert colleagues to situations that have the potential to end badly. There is power in pushing back in real time.

I'll give you an example. Early in my career I learned to take meetings, for network purposes and to grow my career, any chance I got. And I would encourage all young women to take meetings with people who can help you grow and develop. It's an important part of advocating for yourself—if anything, to practice speaking about yourself. It's important to meet with people in your field who hold power, like your managers, and to update them on your progress, showing them projects you've worked on, and being able to articulate the value of what you've brought to the table. It's important to find moments to reiterate all the good work you've done. In the course of my career it's something I've done in every job I've had.

In my 30s, in addition to going out to lunches to catch up professionally and networking with managers and network executives, I also made the decision to go out for drinks with them. Sometimes lunch or brunch was not possible; it was easier to say, "Let's meet after work."

To my mind, it was an opportunity to be time-efficient. I never felt pushed by anyone who offered to grab drinks after work; I always did so voluntarily. The thinking was, "If I can't have lunch, and I have to file this piece for the evening news, I'll meet you after work for a drink at the bar across the street."

Over drinks with one network executive, I was telling him about some of the stories I was working on, and about how much I loved my job. I wanted him to know the kind of work I was doing, and who I was working with. I was advocating for myself for any potential projects in the pipeline.

In the middle of one meeting over a drink, he asked me if I would do "anything that my husband didn't know about." This was leading to nowhere good.

Without thinking twice about it, I knew this was my red line. This was not something I was comfortable with. In real time, I said, "No, I wouldn't."

And then I looked him very clearly in the eye, making sure I held eye contact, and very directly said: "Listen, I like you and enjoy talking to you. And I've learned a lot. I hope I can continue to do my job and flourish. This should work out as friends. I really love my job and hope I can continue to do it and do it well."

There was an awkward silence. Yes, it was uncomfortable. He was embarrassed. But I let that breathe. He got the message.

We ended the night very nicely. I went home, and I even felt a little bad that I went for drinks. But here is the thing: it wasn't my fault. I didn't ask him to ask that question. But I did have to acknowledge that the environment might have invited that type of thing. I own that. In the future, I always had lunch with him instead.

Two days after the awkward meeting over drinks, I asked him, "Hey, can we grab lunch? I'm going to be out of town the next couple of weeks, but I'd love to follow up on my career and on my job." I made sure he saw that I was okay, and that we could move forward and turn the page. Ultimately, I was promoted to a big job by this executive; we both moved on from that uncomfortable situation. I was never punished for it.

As I write this, I absolutely understand there are women who have not been as fortunate, women who are structurally at a disadvantage and fear speaking out. Women whose demurrals will result in real repercussions. But in the past few years, we have seen woman after woman speak out and regain power over situations they're uncomfortable with.

Across the board, there is less tolerance for inappropriate behavior. This is only the beginning, and there certainly is much more work to do. But there has never been a more promising time for women, and for men, for that matter, to feel safe and protected in the workplace when speaking out against people or situations that make them feel uncomfortable.

But we must get better at speaking out in the moment; we've got to do our part. I will say that I'm concerned when I hear stories of women being asked by a network executive or a big media person to go out for drinks, and that they can't find the words if it gets inappropriate. You've got to know what your red lines are and speak out when they are crossed.

Another thing women, especially young women, can do, is to be aware of the situations they're walking into.

Because thinking back, never once was it necessary for me to have drinks. After about the fifth offer to go out for drinks, I realized that not one of those meetings with a network executive was productive for me. All of them ended with a missed cue about the expectations for, or purpose of, the meeting.

Admittedly, there are still many industries, notably in Silicon Valley and on Wall Street, where women might feel real pressure to join the "bros" in out-of-the-office socializing or else be excluded from the cliques that might support advancement in their ranks. It's not uncommon, as unfair as it is. All ambitious women can advocate fiercely for themselves, and as usual, out work and out think the competition. It's pointless and counter-productive to try to be "one of the boys."

For the 2018 re-release of my *Knowing Your Value* book, I spoke to Senior Vice President of Human Resources for Independence Blue Cross, Jeanie Heffernan. We discussed the importance of understanding the purpose of a meeting in this context.

It's worth mentioning again, as Jeanie noted, "It's always helpful to have clarity: Why are we there? What are we trying to accomplish? What are the expected outcomes? Whoever is being invited to the session should be clear about the purpose and the intended outcomes, so the meeting doesn't end up in awkwardness of some sort. You want everyone to understand the meeting is for business purposes and not a social situation."

As an example, she described a time when a board member she worked with reached out for lunch and wanted to introduce her to another man. She wasn't very close to the board member, so she thought, "This is a little sensitive." She knew that because he was someone in power, she needed to manage the politics of it, but also needed to be clear on what she was getting herself into. What was the purpose of the meeting?

So she sent back this response: "I am happy to do this, can you help me understand what the purpose of the lunch is? What is it you need from me? What is your hope of the outcome of this introduction to this gentleman?"

By asking this, she allowed herself to avoid a potentially uncomfortable situation. When you follow her example, you also allow yourself to be purposeful and time-efficient. As you grow in your career, you should make sure all meetings have an explicit intention. It ensures that as you are growing your value in your career, you're also being effective in meeting with people who bring YOU value.

As Jeanie says, it also better prepares you to bring the proper reflections or input to the table, so it's thought-out and you aren't just in "reactionary mode." You can project yourself in an informed, professional way. You're setting yourself up to advocate for your side more effectively.

I do think the part of the conversation we own is how we handle a missed cue. A missed cue can also go both ways: a man likes a woman at work, and she doesn't like him back; but they still work together. Or a woman can have a crush on the man or have inappropriate intentions toward him, and he doesn't reciprocate. Those things happen in the world. Women need to be prepared for human interactions when we go to work.

At the same time, corporations and companies need to do their part. And many have listened and started to implement a zero-tolerance policy against sexual harassment. Better workplace cultures are in the making. And women should be empowered to speak up.

And using your voice doesn't just apply to situations in which you are being treated inappropriately. You should feel empowered to use your voice any time you feel demeaned or devalued, as when more assertive male colleagues try to take credit for your ideas, or in situations where someone is abusing you. This includes being paid less than the men in your workplace.

You should feel empowered to use your voice any time you feel
demeaned or devalued.

Following Your Gut

Your red line can also just be a situation in which your gut is
telling you something. It's either flagging you to push back on an
uncomfortable situation, or it's telling you to speak out on something you feel strongly about. That red line can sometimes goad
you into following through on a decision, despite it being against
the belief of a group telling you otherwise. Women need to pay
close attention to this, because it can lead to valuable opportunities
for growth.

Emily Jane Fox describes the power of advocating from your
gut—sticking to a decision despite resistance: "Sometimes it's
hard as a female reporter. A lot of editors or reporters are men,
and they may have different ideas about what their gut is telling
them. Even if they have more experience than you, you need the
courage to say, 'I don't want to do that,' or 'I think this is better,'
or 'My gut is telling me this.'"

For a young woman like Emily, it takes courage to do
that—to speak out in real time. "But I've always done that,
and I have a good track record. But the first time you do it,
you're putting yourself out there and a lot of self-doubt can
seep in. You just have to swallow it and say, 'I'm going to do
it anyway.'"

Her advice to young women who are struggling to find their
voice in the workplace is: "You have to own who you are and

where you are; then I think that people will respect you for being authentic."

Advancing in your career starts with coming to terms with the fact that you are your own best advocate, showing your ambition effectively, having confidence in acting on your convictions (and practicing saying it out loud!), and knowing when to say that something doesn't feel right in real time. These are all things that strengthen and give power to your voice. Working on all of this will build you from the inside out to prepare for the next step: getting what you're worth.

CHAPTER SEVEN

NEGOTIATING 101

You've been in your job for a while, long enough to hit your stride. You're getting your work done efficiently, supporting the team and making real contributions to the company's goals and bottom line. At this point you want to start keeping a record of your achievements, because it's time to start figuring out what those contributions are worth—and making sure you're compensated appropriately.

As of 2018, women still make 80 cents for every dollar a man makes. An analysis conducted by the National Partnership for Women & Families found that on average, women employed full-time in the United States lose a combined total of nearly $900 billion every year due to the wage gap.

More than one-quarter (29 percent) of young women between 18 and 30 do not believe they are paid fairly compared to others in their company in similar roles (Harvard Kennedy School IOP, Spring 2018 survey).

The research also showed that young adults from minority

backgrounds are hit the hardest. Young men and women who are white are significantly more likely to believe they are paid fairly compared with Hispanics and Asians.

My advice to young women? It's time to work hard and get ahead, and it's also time we get smart and strategic about closing that wage gap. While equal pay is still a problem across many sectors of the job market, and many of the forces that keep wages inequal are still in place, we don't have to simply accept the status quo. There are steps you can take, and tactics you can employ, that can bridge the gap.

Step one: Young women have to feel comfortable asking to be compensated appropriately.

Our Harvard research shows that 75 percent of millennial women between 20 and 29 do not feel confident negotiating their salary.

My Missed Moment

If you've been working hard for the first few years of your career, you want to be ready to talk about what value you bring to your job. You don't want to miss that crucial moment. I missed the moment when I first came to *Morning Joe*—I signed a contract because I was just grateful to get it. I should have paused to consider the fact that I was helping to bring in great ratings numbers, and that it gave me real leverage.

Afterward I looked around at the guys who were not coming to work until they had contracts to their liking. They were cutting huge deals, and I had totally missed my opportunity to get my value in real time. But I'm not alone: I think women have a harder time owning what they're really worth. Please learn from my mistakes: if you're in business and starting to work alongside professionals who make a lot more money than you, or who have much higher titles but do the same work you do, be ready to seize your moment.

> ...if you're in business and starting to work alongside professionals who make a lot more money than you, or who have much higher titles but do the same work you do, be ready to seize your moment.

Use the Data

The simplest and most effective way to be paid what you're worth is to make sure you know the going rate for the work you do. Arm yourself with data when it comes to your salary. Research average salaries in your field, and for your position. When you know what others make for the same work, it's easier to ask for a raise—because you're not asking for any favors, you're just asking for the going rate.

Nowadays, there are more technological tools than ever to give you information on average salaries in your field. To start, you can look at the Occupational Outlook Handbook—

a all-encompassing resource guide published by the U.S. Department of Labor's Bureau of Labor Statistics, that breaks down average salary based on industries. O*NET OnLine allows you to explore salaries based on geographic location or ZIP Code.

Other resources include the NACE Salary Calculator the and Glassdoor Salary Database on Glassdoor.com. Other websites like Vault.com, Payscale.com, and Salary.com are also useful tools. There are even phone apps that help uncover what people around you earn, like Dice Careers from Dice.com and WageSpot, which help map salaries in your area, estimate your salary worth based on skill and location, and even identify how you might increase your earning potential.

Also—talk to people. Talk to people in your industry, both men and women, about what they think the range of salaries is for people in your field, and in your position. Salaries can vary significantly, and the more you know, the better prepared you are.

Negotiating your compensation is so important—especially at the beginning of your career. Raises are typically a percentage improvement over your existing salary. If your existing salary is under market, what does that mean? It means you're always going to be underpaid unless you push. When you're gearing up for that first salary negotiation, executive coach Liz Bentley says to always go in asking for a number that's higher than what you expect to get, especially because young women are often paid below market value. And if you know you're paid below market rate, she says, you should ask for a salary marketplace adjustment.

We have to get out of our comfort zone when it comes to asking for money. Feeling the burn and pressure when you're advocating for yourself is important. The more you do, you'll start getting used to it, and the better you'll be at it!

Consider Your Timing

As a former manager, Joanna Coles offers some insight: "If you got a raise three months ago, asking for another one right away is not okay. For most businesses, that feels like too soon. If you've been there a year and you feel that you are entitled to a raise, and you've had a good year, you can present your work. I really urge you to do your research and pull together everything that you have achieved to present it."

Assuming you've paid your dues, bring all the data to the table about WHY you deserve what you're asking for: cite the progress you've made to back it up. Make it clear you've done your research and have a clear rationale for why your salary should be improved.

That means compiling a list of accomplishments you've achieved, and how those efforts have helped the company. Have you found ways to cut costs, or achieve more with less? Have you found new clients, or found new sources of revenue, or played a key role in helping your team do that? Think of how your contribution has improved the bottom line and be as specific as you can with your examples.

Assuming you've paid your dues, bring all the data to the table about WHY you deserve what you're asking for: cite the progress you've made to back it up. Make it clear you've done your research and have a clear rationale for why your salary should be improved.

Now you're prepared—but how do you pick your moment? Clearly you want to have your discussion when you're at a moment of strength—after you've had a notable, visible success, ideally just as the company is planning the budget for their next fiscal year. But few moments are perfect, and salary discussions can be ongoing. Patricia Langer, formerly of NBCUniversal, says, "To me, the most important thing is to be able to step back and reflect on your impact, the value you've brought to the organization. And not bring it as 'therefore at this moment, I want more money,' but more as a continuing conversation. It's fine to say, 'Here's what I've done, what I'd like to do. I'd like you, my manager, to keep all of this in the back of your mind as merit increases come up and as bonuses are paid.'…If you do it that way, really thoughtfully and rationally, and use your influencing skills, you have a shot at getting a higher salary at the right moment in time; but you can't just go in and demand more. It's got to be a work in progress."

Your annual performance review is usually the time when you can present all your accomplishments and achievements. But many companies have already set their budgets by the time performance reviews happen, so that's why making your salary an ongoing discussion can be advantageous.

Patricia adds, "The other thing millennials have to keep in mind is they need to be realistic. They can't expect much higher compensation if that isn't what is typically paid for a particular job. You might think you are incredibly invaluable and worth much more, but if the market, meaning internal competitors and external, is paying a lower amount, you're not likely to get what you're looking for."

And on timing, she agrees with Joanna Coles: "To do it after three months or six months doesn't make any sense to me. It's got to be based on a body of work."

At the Negotiating Table

Dia Simms of Combs Enterprises feels that skills in negotiation are so important that they should be taught in every high school: "It should be required for freshmen in high school: Negotiations 101."

Dia advises women to take time to assess before going into serious negotiations: "Write down your dream outcome and the least you will accept. Practice in front of a mirror. Your body language matters. It needs to be in lock-step with the words you are saying."

The same lessons on interviewing successfully by using effective body language apply here. Are you leaning in and standing up straight? Or are you avoiding eye contact and hunching over? Use your body language and cues to demonstrate confidence and power.

The second piece of effective negotiation, Simms argues, is making it clear you understand the value of the exchange: "What value are you going to offer in exchange for what that person is going to give you? It cannot be a one-sided negotiation.

"You cannot depend on the other person to negotiate for you, and you don't want to end up negotiating against yourself."

Avoid things that will diminish your negotiating power—like saying too much. Make your ask and then embrace the silence. Zip it. Let them do the talking. Don't talk them out of your ask— a sure way to negotiate against yourself.

—DIA SIMMS

Be prepared by taking your research and sticking to a number that makes sense to you. You have your own best interests in mind. The job of the person in front of you is to try to negotiate down. What is the lowest you are willing to accept? Go in with a backup plan.

Avoid things that will diminish your negotiating power— like saying too much. Make your ask and then embrace the silence. Zip it. Let them do the talking. Don't talk them out of your ask—a sure way to negotiate against yourself, as Dia notes.

And it's not enough to say you want or deserve it, she says. "It needs to be very well rooted in the contributions you've made to the company. Make sure you bear in mind the macro and micro implications. What's happening in your industry? What is the supply/demand in your area?"

Simms suggests you make clear how you will make the raise a worthwhile investment for the company. "[You can say,] 'Here's what I will do, and this is how I can add additional value.' Make your argument irrefutable. Make it logic-based, make it sound, but also make it so that the other person understands how they will shine as a result.

"Unfortunately, very often I see people negotiate in one way: 'I deserve this.' And that is, almost ten out of ten times, weak and ineffectual. It doesn't work."

When you're negotiating or advocating for your next step, the tone you bring into the negotiation is also important.

One thing that won't work in your favor? Cindi Leive, former editor in chief of *Glamour,* explains: "Anger never really works in a negotiation—or rarely. If someone has acted in an egregious way, then your anger is very appropriate and should be expressed. But if you're actively negotiating—talking about your salary, your desire to get to the next level—try to talk as dispassionately as possible. This might mean trying to have the conversation earlier, before you're feeling like 'I can't go into this job another day.' By the time you feel like that, you've left it too long."

Instead of coming in with a negative, "I'm frustrated, I'm not happy with the situation," say, "I love what I've done. I just feel like I'm not finding a way to communicate effectively to you exactly how much of this I own. I'd like to give it a try."

The other thing that never works in a negotiation is bringing your personal factors into the equation. Jane Park of Julep Beauty shares: "I've had people sit down and say, 'I need a raise because I bought a house.'"

This never works. That's the wrong approach. All Jane was thinking was, "How's that problem? We didn't buy the house. Your personal budgeting does not impact us."

Park offers an alternative route in dialogue: "I want to stay, but I know that I could be making X at these other places because I have all these skills. I want to be here, I want to contribute here, I know I could make a difference here. How do you help me feel happy every day coming into work here, and not like I'm being undervalued?"

One of the things that women need to be prepared for, and even comfortable with, is getting a "no." We have to be okay with being turned down. It doesn't mean you can't do something about it and go find a "yes" somewhere else outside your company. Just don't take it personally, because that will deter you from doing it again and putting yourself out there.

One of the things that women need to be prepared for, and even comfortable with, is getting a "no." We have to be okay with being turned down.

Joanna Coles advises: "It doesn't mean that you can't go back and ask again in three months, and that's where men are much better than women; they don't take it as personally. It's okay to keep asking. Just do it respectfully and don't give up and don't be sorry if someone says no. Just think to yourself and put it in your diary, "I'm going to ask in three months. 'No' just means 'not yet.'"

When to Ask for a Promotion, Not Just a Raise

Executive coach Liz Bentley was once training a group of employees at a big bank, in a room composed of almost 100 millennials.

All bright, with promising futures: most were Stanford, Yale, Princeton, and Harvard grads. When the topic of "when to ask for a promotion" came up, she asked the new recruits in the crowd to raise their hands if they thought it was a good idea to ask for a promotion. Not surprisingly, almost all the hands went up.

Then Bentley asked them to raise their hands if they thought it was a bad idea to ask for a promotion within six to twelve months into a job. The only hands that went up were the millennial managers in the back of the room.

She describes what she said then to the crowd: "We have a room full of people who have never worked in this business before as full-time employees. This is their first real job. Do you think there is any manager or boss at this very high-end bank who doesn't know you want a promotion, who doesn't think you want to get ahead, who thinks you want to stay in this position for the rest of your career? Do you think there is anyone that doesn't recognize you're trying to work hard and go up the ladder?"

A crowd of confused young professionals looked back at her. "They were all looking at me like, 'What are you talking about?'

"Now let's look at it this way. Say you're the manager, and there are six people that work for you, and all six are asking for a promotion: how does that feel?"

"The fact of the matter is, if you were hired just six months ago into an entry-level job, the employer still needs a warm body in that position. And chances are, there isn't a slot above for you—let alone everyone who was hired at the same time you were—to move into."

The lesson here is to think from the perspective of your employer. Liz adds: "While at a certain point in your career, you may need to ask for your needs to be met, this is far and few between. More often, you should wait to be asked. Millennials in the workplace need to be conscious of the environment around them, because every single one of these super-ambitious, highly talented, incredibly intelligent people that were in the room with me that day all wanted to ask for a promotion in the first six to twelve months. None of them thought that was inappropriate."

Obviously, you can and should have conversations about advancement, but you can ease into them. Liz Bentley suggests: "What's the career track here, or what would it look like for me if I wanted to advance? How do you see things going over the next three years?"

Christina Hall of LinkedIn says, "I never think it's too early for an employee to think about how they could be developing more, contributing more, learning more, expanding, transforming their career. That is very different from coming into a job and asking, 'How soon can I be promoted?' I think, if I were giving someone advice who is new in their career, I would say to think a lot about how I am developing myself and, at the same time, enriching my company at the start before I start asking what they can do for me."

In terms of timing, Patricia Langer, formerly of NBCUniversal, advises that a year to two years is fair game when it comes to considering asking for a promotion: it should never be before a year. It should probably be more like two years, but it depends on the job, the situation, and sometimes whether someone was brought in on a higher salary level, with the expectation that they won't get a big increase for a while.

Jane Park reminds young women of this important fact: "It's much easier for me to think about promoting someone when they come to me with a track record of results: as in, 'Look at all these important contributions I made to the company.' That's a hard one to deny because we want the same things."

Jane asks you to consider this when it comes time for that next step: "Here's the thing: you want me to be here, and I want to be here, so how do we solve this problem together? These are the important criteria, this is how we're going to make this happen. What can you do to help me make this happen?"

At the end of the day, companies want to keep and retain talented people. Jane adds: "It doesn't mean they're always going to be good at it, or they're not biased or all of those other things—but fundamentally, almost every good company wants to keep and promote really good people. Your interests and their interests are aligned; you have to make that visible."

Making your ambition obvious is entirely on you. Young women often think that their desire to take on more and advance to the next level is somehow very obvious to everyone. But guess what? Your boss isn't a mind-reader!

Joanna Coles found this to be one of the most useful insights early on in her own career: "Especially when you are young and just starting out, your own thoughts are incredibly loud in your own head, but nobody else hears them. No one else knows that you are desperate for a job that just opened up. You're just sitting there screaming, 'Look, what about me!' but not actually saying it out loud—because it's often hard to say it out loud, because you might fail."

You've got to say it: use your voice!

That's why learning how to use your voice effectively to ask what you want—concisely, data-driven, and articulately—has to be part of the equation. You have to OWN your voice and make it work for you.

Anjali Sud, CEO of Vimeo (at the age of 34!), has mastered the art of advocating for herself effectively. She rose to CEO of Vimeo, which is the world's largest ad-free online video platform, after just three years at the company, and is now the youngest chief executive of any IAC (InterActiveCorp) brand. Anjali says she made it to the top by delivering results, strategically advocating for herself, and being the kind of teammate who earned trust internally across all levels.

When it comes to raising her hand and asking for bigger opportunities, Anjali did so intently, and has done so with every job she's held: "I don't think I've ever been promoted without advocating for myself. If you don't believe you deserve a bigger opportunity or role, you can't expect others to believe it. You need to be purposeful and selective in advocating. Sometimes young people feel pressure to constantly, continuously advocate, to shout about their contributions from the rooftops. I didn't do that."

Instead of repeatedly going to her boss and saying she wanted a bigger role or a raise: "I waited until I had delivered results for the business. And I've done that my entire career. Think of your career just like any other negotiation—you want to maximize your leverage. You're likely to have a better outcome if you do that. So if you're going to advocate for yourself, do it at a time when you can point to actual results."

In her case, the right time to discuss a broader role was when the division Anjali led had just had its best quarter of accelerated revenue growth. "That's the time to say I'm delivering the goods; now I'd like more responsibility or more recognition."

Here is her advice for young women asking for more at work: "Be as strategic about your career and when you negotiate as you would be about anything else. I haven't found that always asking for more is particularly successful.

> **I have found that being generous in your peer relationships is quite an effective way of supporting your own career goals.**
> **—ANJALI SUD**

"The other thing I found to be effective is investing a lot in my peers and peer relationships. I didn't realize the benefit it would have down the line. I'm a collaborative person; I really respect and enjoy working with my peers. We have a very collaborative culture at Vimeo. Over time, those peers became my advocates. Ultimately, that internal support was critical for my ability to successfully transition to CEO. These colleagues were my peers, and some of them my bosses, and suddenly I became their boss. To make that transition work you have to have earned the respect of the team.

"They have to be the ones saying, 'Hey, why don't you give Anjali this opportunity, she's doing the work.' This was something I didn't realize early in my career: the more that you can be genuinely useful to your peers and help them succeed, the more it's good for the company, and down the line it can also be really good for you and your career. I have found that being generous in your peer relationships is quite an effective way of supporting your own career goals."

Cathy Engelbert, CEO of Deloitte, took every opportunity in her career to diversify her skill set before finally leading the entire company.

For Cathy, Deloitte was her first job out of college; and like a true jack of all trades, she started from the bottom and made her way all the way to the top, as the first female CEO of the consulting giant.

"One of the biggest things I did to advocate for myself was to raise my hand for different opportunities, to build my capabilities that maybe, again, back then I didn't realize I was building. That actually gave me a nice platform to ultimately become the CEO. I never aspired to a box or title called CEO, but I aspired to lead. And through that, the way I led was to raise my hand and say I want to build on something different."

She rotated through many departments of Deloitte, knowing that becoming an expert in different areas would diversify her pool of knowledge, something that is vital for leadership.

"I became a derivative financial instrument expert, then I went into our consulting practice for four years. What I didn't realize was those were the risks I was taking early in my career, to build a broader set of networks and capabilities so that when it came time for a new CEO at Deloitte, I was a part of pool of people that have been developed. I always say I was an outcome of an inclusive culture, not picked because I was in a corporate group."

Those risks included deciding that she wanted to try new things in the company and advocating for herself to serve big clients to build recognition. Her strength came at first from building a niche around a technical area, which in her world translated as derivatives, an area that made her indispensable. Then, when she knew her skills created a niche around a solution, she put herself out there—she again raised her hand and asked to try new things.

Cathy has been incredibly successful at her job by negotiating for more and better opportunities on the job, and when the time came, she also negotiated space to accommodate her home life. "When I was pregnant with my second child, I asked to come back to audit, because I viewed that as more stable. With a second child on the way, I said it was time for me to settle back down and ratchet down the travel.

"I raised my hand for opportunities at different parts in my life, when I felt like I could do something different. And then when I felt that I needed to think about a different way of working, I raised my hand again and said I'd like some flexibility."

Finding your voice and learning to advocate for yourself means getting a chance to innovate and change the status quo. But it starts with raising your hand.

Changing the Role of the Workplace

Cindi Leive notes that we see young women reflecting on the struggles of the previous generation who have vowed to do things differently: "I think a lot of young women in particular feel like the workplace—the traditional workplace—has not necessarily always worked out that well for their mothers or their older sisters. They see pay gaps and women forced to choose between taking care of their kids and having a satisfying career."

Younger generations don't have the blind faith in institutions that my generation did. They have less tolerance for it. "They saw their parents lose their jobs in the recession; we're now seeing all these institutions crumbling thanks to the #MeToo movement. Young women are not as likely to go along just because the person at the top says you have to go along," Cindi adds.

And that's a good thing. While there are challenges ahead as younger women navigate their early career steps, there is also a tremendous opportunity to make a difference—to be ambitious and courageous in their career goals.

Advocating for an Equal Playing Field

Part of the message of this book is learning to navigate the hierarchy of the workplace. The other equally important message is for you to own your voice, and to learn how to advance and advocate for yourself—and, by extension, the next generation of women. Their possibilities and opportunities for advancement will be paved by women currently in the workplace. But it takes each of you to make it happen.

A great example of young women standing up for what is right and finding ways to advocate effectively are hockey gold medalists Monique Lamoureux-Morando and Jocelyne Lamoureux-Davidson, who were part of the U.S. team that threatened a boycott over unequal pay ahead of the IIHF Women's World Championship game in 2017. They acted specifically with the goal of improving things for the next generation of athletes.

In a statement, team captain Meghan Duggan said, "We are asking for a living wage and for U.S.A. Hockey to fully support its programs for women and girls and stop treating us like an afterthought.

"We have represented our country with dignity and deserve to be treated with fairness and respect."

The twins stuck to their guns, even if they had a world championship gold medal on the line: "Ultimately, there was a fear that maybe this wouldn't work out—that they might replace us. But we were confident that with the teammates we had, we were going to make some positive changes," Jocelyne says.

Her sister, Monique, agrees: "We knew we had the right group to make big changes. And we also knew that players in the past tried to do what we had done and didn't achieve it. If we weren't willing to stand up and say something and do what was right, then how could we expect the next generation to do that?"

Both understand the drastic measures they employed to prove the point of fairness in pay. Jocelyne says, "In some cases, you have to take a stand in a dramatic fashion."

She adds, "It's really important, but people are afraid to talk about it. In our case, we knew exactly how some of the boys' teams were being funded, down to the dollar amount. Ultimately, you have to be educated in the things you think are not fair, and where there might be inequalities. Then you can have the confidence to have that conversation, even though it's scary.

"Sometimes you might not get what you want. Ultimately, it's okay to walk away. I think Monique and I are okay with acknowledging that if the boycott and the negotiations hadn't gone the way they had, we would have retired after the PyeongChang Olympics. But now we're playing under totally different circumstances as far as maternity benefits, financial support, more opportunities to play as a national team. It totally changes our perspective and our future within hockey."

After fifteen months of trying to negotiate and doubling down on the boycott, the U.S. women's hockey team successfully achieved increased pay. This wasn't just a change that benefited the women on the hockey team; it proved to be a huge win for gender equity in sports for generations of women to come.

Whether you are negotiating for more money or for a higher role, you need to think big. I am so excited for the potential of young women and their advancement because it's your generation that has said "enough!" to being treated like second-class citizens in the workplace. It's time to use these tools and ask for what you are worth!

CHAPTER EIGHT

FINDING YOUR PURPOSE

You've been in the workforce for a few years, pushing yourself and taking every opportunity to advance and move forward. You've dedicated so much of your time and focused your energies so intently on your goals, perhaps to the exclusion of other life experiences. At some point you're going to pause and think to yourself: Are the sacrifices I've made in my career so far worth it in the long run? Are the goals I've been striving for still my goals? *What am I doing?* Am I truly happy in this job, or am I treading water? And if I'm miserable, what do I do next? Or as my coauthor, Daniela, points out, many in her generation call it "the millennial midlife crisis."

You're not alone in this. As young women, you're under plenty of pressure, with so many new challenges *and* opportunities facing you today. So many, in fact, that the possibilities to progress in your career and find success can be dizzying.

> **Focus groups conducted by Harvard pollster John Della Volpe indicate that for young professionals, there is a strong sense**

of being overwhelmed. Millennials recognize the sacrifices that their parents made and are torn between making them happy and following their passion. This is especially true for young people who might be the first in their family to graduate college.

In your 20s, you probably have more questions than answers about your career trajectory. You're not alone.

Overall, women are less satisfied with their career progress than men of the same age (Harvard Kennedy School IOP, Fall 2017 Survey).

I discussed this inevitable career angst with Donny Deutsch, a regular on *Morning Joe* and chairman of the multibillion-dollar advertising agency Deutsch Inc.

Millennials and Gen Z, he agrees, are living through a time of incredible uncertainty. They have a wide range of options to do just about anything in the world we live in today: "There's not that basic obvious next step, whether it comes to work, family, or sexuality. In the 1950s and 1960s, the lanes were very clear for women's roles, for men's roles, for workplace roles, for sexual roles, for parenting roles, and each lane keeps getting more and more blurry....If a man can turn his body into a woman, if a president can be a goofy reality star, what can I count on? What is a given?" Donny asks.

Unlike for Boomers and Gen Xers, "The world is more in play in what it looks like and feels like than ever before," he adds.

For many young people, Daniela suggests, there's also the FOMO factor: a fear of missing out on greater opportunities. The pressure to figure out what you're "meant to do" is downright EXHAUSTING.

As I see it, young people in their 20s get bogged down on specific boxes they need to check off. But it's important to remember that not everything goes in a straight line. Let me emphasize that your 20s will be full of fluid experiences in the workplace. Put this time of your life in context. You may think you should be leapfrogging upward at this point, because all the pressures we place on ourselves make us think so much time has gone by.

But you have many years to set the tone for your work life. You're not yet halfway through your career—not even close! You are still at the beginning of your life in so many ways.

You may be thinking about starting a family, maybe getting married, don't have any prospects in that department yet, or you're single and trying to focus on you. Whatever it may be, you have a million things going on in your 20s. You are trying to figure it all out and feeling like you are up against the clock. And that spills over to the pressures of your career.

But you have many years to set the tone for your work life. You're not yet halfway through your career—not even close! You are still at the beginning of your life in so many ways.

Daniela and I discussed this vulnerable moment in a young woman's work life. The beginning of her career was devoted to fighting obstacles to get a foot in the door and then effectively navigating those early years. As she approaches her late 20s, the pressure is no longer on getting her start, but on whether she's headed in a meaningful direction.

"Some people's careers are growing faster than others, especially when technology is changing the way you can chart your career. It can create unprecedented and unique opportunities for advancement. Yet it doesn't necessary happen at the same rate or in the same way for everyone. That can feel intimidating—like you're missing out, or falling behind somehow. You've got to constantly remind yourself that your career is yours alone and that your development should happen in your own time."

Now you're in a place where you can emotionally and intellectually take some chances with your ideas and with your ability to communicate at work. Take some risks with your presentation and see if you can find different ways to be heard in your present job.

But don't feel constrained because of the opportunities going to the person next to you. Everyone's thinking, "Oh my gosh, at this point I should be getting tapped for the next step!" Well, one of the reasons you may not be is that you haven't found a way to stand out yet. Or your ideas may not be fully developed. And that's OKAY! We all grow at different paces. We all find that voice at different times.

I learned early on that career comparison is nothing but an energy-sucker. The best thing you can do is turn to yourself.

Focus on what is holding YOU back and what's in your control, then work on it.

Saying Yes Is Good, Until It Isn't

For this book, we asked young women in the workplace what was at the root of their unhappiness as they moved along in their careers: Why did you feel stalled? What are the things holding you back from growing in your career? The sentiment we heard most often: "I feel like I'm stuck in my current role."

As women, we're conditioned to value harmony. At the beginning of your career this is great. It opens doors and opportunities to grow. But how long should you agree to everything in front of you before it starts to be self-sabotaging?

There are a few reasons why young women might feel stuck. The most prevalent was that they felt they weren't being heard—that their ideas weren't being acknowledged. They felt sidelined, or as if they weren't being challenged enough in their current role.

As women, we're conditioned to value harmony. At the beginning of your career this is great. It opens doors and opportunities to grow. But how long should you agree to everything in front of you before it starts to be self-sabotaging?

Our research showed that having job security, working for an organization that is stable with good benefits, and having home and work–life harmony is significantly more important for young women than men. **Men place greater emphasis on being** recognized by their peers, having flexibility to work in different parts of the organization, and having an opportunity to travel (Harvard Kennedy School IOP, Fall 2017 Survey).

The predicament in trying to make everything fit into one long-range career plan is that we get stuck in one way of thinking: Follow the rules and do as you're told. Don't push back, or you'll be seen as difficult. But if you've paid your dues, it's important to keep tabs on how you're doing and where you're going. For example, a prevalent worry we heard from women five years into their jobs was being stuck with administrative tasks that made it harder for them to move up.

If you've been doing well in your career thus far, you've probably been taking on responsibilities that are greater than the administrative tasks you're doing. You've probably been doing both for a while, as you prove yourself, and find a way to be needed for them. As Rebecca Minkoff and Dia Simms pointed out in earlier chapters, there is so much value in young employees who take sometimes unglamorous work and do a great job.

But if several years have passed, and you are still doing work that prevents you from moving forward, that's a different story. If you've been taking every opportunity to say "yes" to the higher-level tasks, but you're still weighed down with administrative tasks, you will have more work thrown at you and end up overwhelmed or, worse, burnt out.

You'll be like Elizabeth Warren, who shared in *Knowing Your Value* that as a professor at Harvard, she would find herself agreeing to teach the classes all the male professors had refused.

She chalked it up to her being a natural cooperator. Someone needed to do the shifts with lousy hours; she'd raise her hand and volunteer. And for women who are making valuable contributions at a point in their career when they can handle more, they should also consider the point when they can also say "no."

But I want to be very cautious with this, because when you are still in your building-block years, you certainly don't want to miss out on opportunities or make it seem like you don't want to work hard. You want to be far enough along in your career to know when taking lower-level jobs is hurting your progress, not helping it.

This is a pervasive problem for women specifically. We are natural people-pleasers. As women, we've got to take stock of when we are making contributions with no valuable return.

It's a time to practice using your voice. It's a time to sit down with your boss, discuss your goals, and highlight the great things you're doing that are part of your long-range plan.

It's a time to practice using your voice. It's a time to sit down with your boss, discuss your goals, and highlight the great things you're doing that are part of your long-range plan.

But you also have to understand the needs of the business you're working in and how the work is being divided. Is there room to grow or does the structure of your company limit your capacity to expand on other skills? Can you do the work that is required of you while taking extra work that will take you to the next level? You should do both until the higher-level tasks are part of the promotion that (hopefully!) you asked for.

When you start working on the projects, assignments, or duties you want, are there tasks that are slowing you down? Maybe it's time to have a conversation with your boss about task division within your department. Give yourself a time limit to have that conversation. Depending on the structure of your company, administrative tasks might stay with you as you move on to the next level if you don't work at a company that is sufficiently staffed. Assess if this is something that is slowing down the work that will advance you.

For example, when Daniela came to me to pitch her next step, she had a full plate. She was only two years into her job and was essentially doing the jobs of four people. She was the main show producer in the mornings in the studio, running point for all guests; she was managing our entry-level staff and interns; she was traveling as a logistics producer for remote shows; and she acted as a part-time show booker.

She would be managing the set and escorting guests. Then, if we needed to book a last-minute guest for breaking news, she'd be on the phone waking up experts in one hand, and on hold with car services for show logistics on the other. She was staffing me at events and speaking engagements, adding "unofficial part-time assistant" to her title. She'd be answering emails at 10 p.m. for show guests and their publicists, and then would get up at 3:30 a.m. to do it all over again.

Exposed to high-level assignments from the start, Daniela was also entrusted with tons of administrative work, like managing the office, and making sure our office closets were curated with the right clothes to help put together our on-air outfits. And she did all those things simultaneously, working directly with show guests and building her network of talent contacts while also doing the menial tasks.

But when she got a sense that the time was right—on both the show-needs side (you shouldn't leave things hanging that need to be done) and in proving herself by taking up more complex tasks, she spoke up about the opportunities she sought.

Daniela volunteered for everything starting out and did the grunt work; but she was able to pivot to a higher role at *Morning Joe* because she managed to say "yes" strategically. As she slowly moved up, she continued to do the lower-level work, until one day it was clear that she had the next step figured out. And by then, there was someone less senior who could take on those tasks. While our show had a smaller staff, Daniela didn't complain or think twice about doing all the work that needed to be done. But she learned the power of delegating and knowing when to say, "In order to do this part of my job effectively, I have handed off this administrative task to so-and-so."

For this reason, it's important to use your voice to create the change you want for yourself and get to the next level. As Joanna Coles mentions in an earlier chapter, no one knows what you're thinking. When it's time, speak up!

Growing Your Brand Strategically

That professional persona or brand that you would have been working hard to polish is going to come in handy when you look for ways to leverage opportunities for your career.

I wish I had known that sooner.

For a big chunk of my career, I didn't have an immediately identifiable brand. I didn't have anything that would identify my perspective, personal style, and professionalism. I had a boxed view of what a television news reporter was supposed to be and look like. I was stuck on the stereotype of what is meant to be a reporter; I wanted to do everything that was asked of me. I found myself spread thin going from deadline to deadline, from live shot to live shot.

At one point, it felt like I was just going through the motions. My network news job was pulling me in a ton of different directions at once.

I got a wake-up call one day when my daughter Carlie was an infant. As I stepped into my daughter's room to pick her up, I was zipping around talking nonstop, not paying close enough attention as I approached the stairs. I reached into my pocketbook to do the usual payment to the nanny when I miscalculated my step. Next thing I knew, I was flying down the staircase—with my daughter in my arms! I crashed mid-stairs, managing to hold on to her. We raced to the hospital. It was nothing short of a miracle that we ultimately ended up all right after Carlie healed from a broken leg. I was devastated. Hysterical.

My guilt was paralyzing. It was a heart-stopping moment.

That tragedy wouldn't have happened if it weren't for factors like fatigue, the pressures I had placed on myself—real or imagined—from work, or if I hadn't been overextended, overwhelmed, exhausted, and reeling, trying to juggle too much.

My network news job was demanding and grueling. Doing and taking all the opportunities that had come my way was working to my detriment.

What I really needed was time to slow down. After building my career from the ground up, I needed to take time to figure out what I liked doing and how I could *strategically* grow my value and professional persona, instead of just riding the waves and following everywhere I was told to go. It was time for me to make decisions that didn't leave me feeling spread thin and mentally depleted.

You might be thinking, "I thought I was supposed to start my career and work around the clock and take all the opportunities in front of me??" Trust me: you absolutely should! Those first years are the dogged years to do everything you can to gain leverage to ask for the things you want. But young women need to be vigilant about when to ask for more and start making strategic decisions to grow. You need to build leverage first. For those who have more questions than answers about where they want their careers to go, this is important.

There was a time in my career where I was just taking tons of different jobs on air without focus. I was reacting to opportunities instead of advocating for myself and taking the time to pitch what would grow my brand. But it took me a while to figure that out. I needed to assess what was holding me back from growing myself purposefully instead of just riding the ebb and flow of opportunities in front of me.

Dealing with a Negative Environment

What if you feel like you are in the middle of an environment that is difficult to navigate? Perhaps you have an "impossible" boss who you feel sidelined by, and makes you feel 'stuck.' Remember the lessons about all experiences being good for your growth? Yes—it certainly isn't pleasant, but if the work is important to you, you should find a way to overcome it. To see it through.

I asked executive coach Liz Bentley to break down both scenarios and offer a few solutions: "Whenever you feel like you're in a toxic environment, you have to first look at yourself."

> The only person we're working on is ourselves. Any time we distract ourselves with complaining and blaming other people, we are thinking about how they need to change instead of thinking about what we need to do to grow ourselves.
>
> —LIZ BENTLEY

The first thing Liz advises her clients to do in these situations is to consider an honest self-assessment. You might feel like your boss is pushing your buttons maliciously, but in truth, your boss may have valid reasons to be unhappy with you.

To clarify, she notes, "The only person we're working on is ourselves. Any time we distract ourselves with complaining and blaming other people, we are thinking about how they need to change instead of thinking about what we need to do to grow ourselves."

"A boss who's impatient and demanding may seem critical and unfair, but their frustrations may be due to our inadequacies that we need to address."

Ask yourself: Is there something about your performance that can be improved or corrected?

It may be that your boss isn't the best manager, "He or she may have a lot of areas to work on, including their ability to deliver feedback and control their emotions. That is their challenge, not yours, the only part of the equation you control—is YOU. The question you should consider is: What are you doing with the feedback you're getting? If you're getting mad at them, you're not working on yourself," Liz notes.

If your boss is truly toxic—not just to you, but to the entire company—that's another problem. But Liz stresses that even bad jobs can be useful: "Learning how to be able to handle any situation is one of the most valuable skills you can acquire."

She once worked for a woman who was a really tough boss and verbally abusive: "She would yell and throw your work across the room if you made a mistake while cursing at you and telling you that you were terrible. She was mean and demanding!"

Liz told herself: "If I want to get promoted, I have to figure out how to work with this person because she is the gatekeeper to the next job. I need to figure out how not to make mistakes and not make her angry with me."

She acknowledged that while no one should be this demeaning, that was the boss' issue, not hers.

Bentley thought it through and figured out how to empathize with her boss and her position. "Why is she yelling? She's yelling because mistakes cost the company millions of dollars. And back then she was the only female in a top VP position, and she probably had zero support from the men or the women around her. She had a lot of pressure on her to perform and her back was against the wall every single day.

Everyone has a reason for the way they're showing up to their life. By empathizing with the boss' tough role in the company and daily struggles she faced, Liz could reset her mindset and approach the problem from a new vantage point.

Liz stopped making those mistakes: "I worked my ass off, and I became her favorite employee. Not only did I get her approval, I improved my work performance and I even liked her in the end." Bentley got promoted while the other people in her department did not. She considers working for this tough boss "probably one of the best learning experiences of my life. It taught me that if I want to change my situation, I am the one who has to make the shift."

Find Your Moments

Sometimes feeling stuck comes from not recognizing or identifying windows of time to make your pitch for the next step. Liz Bentley puts it like this: "If you're trying to go up the food chain in the work environment, there are windows that open, and you've got to be able to move through them when they do."

Sometimes feeling stuck comes from not recognizing or identifying windows of time to make your pitch for the next step.

She gives the example of starting as an assistant and wanting to get promoted to the next step: you might feel sidelined if you don't move on to more responsibility in year two or three of the job. Assistant work is not supposed to be a career, it's only a stepping stone for the next position. "If there are twenty-five assistants on your floor, and only five are getting promoted, then you need to be one of them. If you're not, you might get sidelined. Then you have to get promoted in the next round or start to look somewhere else for a similar job or do something different."

To help yourself in that situation, Bentley suggests that you ask yourself: 'What are those windows of opportunity and when are those windows open?' and 'Am I positioning myself to get through them?'

"Because there is a time when everyone is looking at you and evaluating you, deciding whether they're going to put you through the window and take you to the next level," she says. To recognize that window, you've got to have your finger on the pulse of the office environment. "You've got to figure out what you can do so that you're in a position to know when openings are coming."

One thing Liz Bentley says might make it hard for you to identify those openings is having a "What's in it for me?" attitude. You are thinking of it the wrong way if you find yourself constantly asking, "'What is the company doing for me?' not 'What am I doing for the company?'" If you start identifying ways to contribute to the team, making things better for your company instead of the other way around, you are pointed in the right direction. Liz adds, "That's the coaching we do to get the aha moments all the time, and that's how you get through the window. You have to be working for the greater good."

Once you perform jobs that will help build your professional persona, it's time to acknowledge what isn't good for your growth in your workplace environment.

Finding Your Purpose

You are part of an incredibly purposeful generation that deeply cares about the impact they leave behind. But what does that mean for your career path and the choices you should make?

Cindi Leive, formerly of *Glamour* magazine, observes of millennials and Gen Z: "They want to work for companies or organizations that are mission-driven. They don't see a distinction between their personal lives and their work lives, so they're looking for personal meaning in their work.

"I think the average 25-year-old, if they have any economic choice about where they work, in what field and company, they're going to choose something that they feel is personally fulfilling to them. They want to feel that the companies and organizations that they work for have some sort of mission. They don't just want to go in and make the widgets, they want to understand how the widgets are making the world better."

Like most other young women, Daniela strongly believes in having a purpose. Her personal mission is to help people who are disadvantaged gain access to opportunities.

Daniela's interest in using her background and skills to affect change is shared by most millennials. Cindi Leive observes of the hundreds of millennials she's managed throughout the years: "They're very interested and invested in their own personal growth and their own personal destiny."

Millennials gravitate toward purpose-driven companies that value accountability and make a social impact. It's great to want to make an impact, but what does that mean, exactly? Leadership expert Simon Sinek points to one of the reasons mission-driven young people become dissatisfied in their quest to find a purposeful career.

"Do you want to help the environment, people, stop world hunger, serve your community? Impact is too broad. You go into the tech space, and every company says they want to make the world a better place. Really, they want you to download their app, so you can order takeout food quicker. This concept of corporate social responsibility has been confused with making an impact.

"Giving a percentage to charity or buy-one-give-one or sponsoring a fun run to raise money for cancer research is not impact. That's charitable, and I think that's wonderful and good. But let's not confuse it. There are plenty of companies that are making a significant impact on the world, but they don't sponsor cancer research. It's the idea of how people feel when they get to work. They are contributing to something bigger than themselves."

Simon cites the example of a company "attempting to redefine capitalism so that it serves the needs of the people and employees more than shareholders. That's impact. Everyone who works there feels that they're a part of something. I think millennials need to be more specific about what 'impact' means to them as individuals.

Right now, it's too broad—and they're making random decisions to work at companies and are then dissatisfied."

Finding my own purpose involved filling in the blanks to get myself in the door of the first few jobs that would expose me to what I liked—and equally important, to what I didn't like, as well as failing. It helped me get closer to defining the level of impact I wanted to make and how. It was also about getting through the awkward moments and learning something about myself along the way. I look back at cringe-worthy moments on the air and chalk them up to learning experiences. But they are necessary for your development and growth. How else will you find out that a certain job or career path just isn't right for you?

Feeling Stuck

Feeling like you are stuck in your role, however you define it, can feel suffocating. But I would encourage you to change your perspective. Look at these moments as productive check-ins with yourself. Take a moment to step back (be cautious about thinking that's the same thing as stepping backward. It's not!) and really assess the situation. Might it be a good thing that you are getting outside your comfort zone and being challenged at your current job? Yes! Even if it doesn't feel completely satisfying right now. Even moments when you wonder, *What am I doing here?* can have value: they're important to take into consideration.

In between my time doing overnights at CBS and getting the job as a CBS News correspondent, I did a show called *HomePage* with Ashleigh Banfield and Gina Gaston in the early 2000s. It was a women's show, on the air for three hours in the afternoon. And boy, did I try to be something I wasn't. On air, I wore snakeskin boots and tight tops; I had chopped-off hair. My knees stuck out of miniskirts. I was unrecognizable.

For those two years I paraded around in short skirts and high boots. It felt uncomfortable, and I was bad at it—horrible, in fact. I was a poser. And I had to go through that to learn and realize what felt good and what felt wrong for my career.

And for two years I did a job that was so not me. I just was trying to be something I wasn't. I decided to go back to CBS because I wasn't comfortable with the product I was putting out there, and the message I was sending. But trying to stick through that job and make it work was important. It helped me figure myself out along the way and get me closer to my purpose.

When I went back to CBS shortly after leaving that afternoon show, and I covered 9/11, I knew I was exactly where I should be.

Covering the 9/11 attack was a moment of true clarity for me. I grew up in a family that debated U.S. foreign policy at the dinner table every night. With this reporting, I was able to incorporate whatever had seeped in by osmosis being the daughter of a national security advisor and combine it with a genuine interest in people and their lives. Being on the ground by the towers, covering the story firsthand, meeting the people who lost family members, reporting on the heroism of the firefighters and the NYPD, and on how suddenly America was changed: suddenly it all clicked.

I knew what I was meant to do.

After 9/11, I never turned my back on hard news again. I

knew I should be covering important stories. It inspired me to hold on to what felt like an intimate fit between me and my job. After many twists and turns, saying yes to opportunities in front of me (even if some were not ideal!), and learning to take risks by trusting my gut to make decisions that perhaps took me a step back, but eventually brought me to where I am now, I've found my purpose after all those years.

The best advice I have for finding your true purpose is BE STILL. Take a moment to think of the skills you're trying to develop. How can you connect what you're doing now to a job that might ultimately make you happy? Does your current job allow you to create a financial blanket for your future career jump? Does it instill technical skills that may seem menial to you in the moment? What about soft skills? Take stock of your current arsenal of skills and build some new ones if you need to.

> **The best advice I have for finding your true purpose is BE STILL. Take a moment to think of the skills you're trying to develop. How can you connect what you're doing now to a job that might ultimately make you happy?**

Here is what you have to ask yourself when you're considering leaving or sticking it out in a tough job: What does your experience at work tell you about yourself? How are you growing your personal and professional tools? Yes, there are the technical tools you need, but what about mental toughness, resilience in working long hours, or dealing with tough situations or coworkers? Those are skills and lessons that you will need as you move up. In fact, the more demanding and ambitious your career goals, the more you'll *really* need these skills.

These experiences in your mid-career are going to make you tough as nails and help you think of the right questions to ask yourself about your career: Am I okay with working in this business, but need a change of culture? Is this the wrong *fit* for me? If so, what feels wrong, exactly?

If the work is unfulfilling, is it at least teaching you an important skill you wouldn't have learned otherwise? How can you stick this out and learn something along the way? This is important especially if you feel a bit directionless in this part of your career trajectory.

There is a lesson in every challenge and opportunity that will help you stop and reflect on your career, rather than going through the motions. You shouldn't feel tied to a certain career path if it's not doing anything for your self-development. But keep in mind that just because things in your career are not manifesting right now—whether you're coming out of college, or in your mid-20s, or approaching your 30s—doesn't mean you'll never get there. Maybe it's time, though, to find a new way to stand out within the parameters of your job.

When it comes to figuring out that next step, of course you are going to feel disillusioned and stuck if you are waiting for it to find you! It's key to develop discipline and to pace yourself, knowing your time will come—as long as you keep trying, taking those risks, and developing your communication skills.

Striving for Success with a Sense of Purpose

So how do you showcase your skills once you've gone through the dogged years? It's good to say yes and raise your hand for everything you can volunteer for, but how do you pivot into getting more from your career?

Daniela is a good example of doing this effectively. She started building her professional persona at *Morning Joe*—developing and growing as a booking producer and building her contacts in and around the industry.

But she was raising her hand for other opportunities to grow into a different phase of her career, using her network of contacts to help book newsmakers and celebrities for network events and projects for my Know Your Value platform. She created peripheral opportunities outside of her normal job on *Morning Joe* to develop her personal brand and work on things she was passionate about on the side.

As she puts it: "I looked for opportunities to do things on my own time to grow myself in different ways. I started pitching and writing pieces for digital publications, volunteered to do red carpets, and got involved with special projects that allowed me to expand my focus outside the politics space. Having a role on Know Your Value and collaborating and working on pieces that highlight women's empowerment is something I've been doing outside of my normal job to advance in a space I feel passionate about. It strikes a personal chord with me."

As you progress in your career and learn to leverage your opportunities at work, you might find new ways to grow outside of your job in order to find your sense of purpose. As you think of ways to grow in your career, you'll have to find effective ways to talk about your professional brand.

Get Rid of Distractions

You can't find your purpose or develop your personal brand if you're relying on outside input only. Young women today are so reactive and dependent on external feedback. It's part of the reason why our self-esteem is so fragile, as broadcaster Katty Kay mentioned: everyone has an opinion, and women try to keep up with what is expected of them. And while it's helpful to get an outsider's point of view, when you're being bombarded by social media and trying to keep up appearances and fit a career trajectory that looks perfect on someone else, you are not working on your own purpose. You become distracted from the most important voice—your own.

There are things in our society that can increase unnecessary noise when we're navigating through confusing times and trying to make a decision while listening to our gut and trying to find ways to build our value. These need our complete, undivided attention.

Harvard pollster and expert on the attitudes of young Americans John Della Volpe has found that his recent conversations and town meetings with high school and college students who are part of Gen Z have taken on a negative, darker tone than the ones he hosted with millennials not that long ago. "Within a few minutes of convening a group of teenagers today, Gen Z students openly begin to speak alarmingly about the negative impact that social media has had on their lives," he told me. "Both young men and women talked about feeling isolated, losing a sense of connection with peers and others due to the divisive nature of most social media platforms.

"The fear of missing out, the fear of being judged, and the concern of committing to relationships were expressed by many who speak glowingly of a simpler time when they were elementary and middle school age, and they could talk, play, hang around, and form the meaningful relationships that many believe are lacking today."

In earlier chapters, we looked at how being in a technology-dependent culture can affect things like our demeanor and even our ability to think deeply and contextually. But what we also found was that always being on our phones can disconnect us from our inner selves—an important part of who we are, how we make connections, how we find inspiration, and how we get to know ourselves better. The women you read about earlier who found great success in their careers relied on their inner compass and gut feelings to guide them. To get in touch with yours, it's important to find ways to pull back from all that overconnecting.

You might take up hobbies: painting, playing music, writing. Or even do small activities that help you de-stress: go on a nature walk or play with your pets. Do whatever you need to find that quiet space! For me it's jogging—it gets me out of my head. If I've had a tough day or am struggling with a decision, it always helps me center my thoughts. Find those moments to inspire yourself. Your future will thank you.

How can you put yourself first and find ways to hear yourself? What are your goals, and what are the distractions that are limiting your ability to get there?

Making the Jump

Daniela and I discussed how hard it is for young women to make a career jump as they approach their late 20s. They almost feel as if they've run out of time. Or they're afraid of starting over.

She explains some of the fears of her generation: "I think this comes from the idea that a career move that turns out not to be the 'right choice' will alter our way ahead—put us off the path of where we want to be, ultimately. And sometimes we don't know what that end goal is. The fear of starting over is paralyzing in terms of rebooting our careers in a new direction. But at the same time, it's important to make the move if we have the gut feeling that what we are doing isn't right."

If you've followed all the steps we've been talking about, and you've opened your mind to learning and absorbing in your first few years; but you've hit a point where you can't possibly imagine doing what you do, know that you can always change course. Perhaps you want to start over with another career entirely. You can do it—but you've got to quiet the voices that are saying that it's too late for you. For young women especially, it's important to know that it's not about losing time if you think it's necessary to reroute your career.

Worst-Case Scenarios

Sometimes starting over in a career is driven not because you feel stuck, or are shoved out, but because you literally can't get yourself to go to a job you hate. That's what happened to Julep Beauty CEO Jane Park, who had a law degree from a top university.

Sometimes starting over in a career is driven not because you feel stuck, or are shoved out, but because you literally can't get yourself to go to a job you hate.

One day she told her husband: "I would rather be hit by a car than go to work." She was completely miserable being an attorney. Somehow, she'd never really thought about how solitary the work could be: "For maybe three months I went without barely having to talk to anybody. It was just me in a room with fifty boxes of documents, looking for evidence." Her husband sensibly told her that, as the holder of two degrees from Ivy League universities, she could find another job.

She recalls: "It was kind of a crazy thing to me: when I stepped back and thought about it, there are so many women who don't speak the language fluently, who don't have the advantages and the degrees I had—and yet I could feel so stuck. It was an incredible realization that being stuck was mainly in my head."

Yet it's perfectly understandable for the daughter of Korean immigrants with a 7-Eleven store: "My dad lost his parents when he was nine. The thought that I could turn my back on the highest-paying job I could get was really hard for me.

"I think one of the things women can do if they're that un-happy is to ask, 'How do you try something different?' knowing that if it doesn't work out, you can always go back. So that was an important thing for me throughout my whole life in trying to find different careers."

When she was feeling really stuck, Jane loved to play the game of "worst-case scenario," as employed by the characters Randall and Beth Pearson on the TV show *This Is Us*. They go back and forth imagining that she might wind up a pole dancer or that they might be homeless.

Jane Park observes: "You realize that the chances of these worst-case scenarios happening are low, and that even the worst-case scenario is survivable. I even did that when I was starting a business: if it failed, I could always go back to a safe corporate job. Women overestimate these scenarios, and we don't talk about them enough.

"You can always go back to the home base where you are comfortable and catch your breath, and then try again."

This assumes, of course, that you've established a home base to begin with: that's where a solid education and experimenting with different jobs comes in, not to mention possible internships where you can observe how the professionals in that field do their work. Stagnating in a comfortable role might be riskier for your growth than taking a real risk. And as I've said before, you gain the confidence to do that once you have some solid skills under your belt. It can take a while.

Vanessa De Luca, formerly of *Essence*, didn't find a happy place in her career until she was 30 years old. She had been working for seven years in retail, as a store manager at Macy's and as a furniture buyer, when she decided to change the trajectory of her career. She wasn't fulfilled in her job, and she knew she wasn't doing what she wanted to do.

But those jobs weren't in vain: they brought her real value and helped leverage the management experience and people skills she'd need down the road. Just after she turned 30, she decided to reinvent her career. She had always wanted to work in a magazine, so she went back to school and got a certificate in magazine publishing over a summer to get in front of a job fair at the end of the course. Eventually, she found a job working as an editorial assistant at *Glamour* magazine.

"I had to go through a couple of other jobs I quite frankly hated, or just didn't feel like the right fit for me, to kind of figure out where I really wanted to land. And then I realized that in order to do that, I was going to have to go back to square one and start over and get paid half as much and move back in with my parents and all that. But I did it because I just knew that it was the right thing to do."

Before getting to where she is now, she had to figure out where she fit in the world, what her skills were. She had to come to understand that her first job was not going to be her dream job—even if she may have not known it was going to pan out that way at the beginning of her career.

Most people thought Vanessa was crazy when she started at a lower level in her 30s, but it paid off—big time. Even after having to start over, Deluca made it all the way to editor in chief.

See what I mean when I say that the idea of losing time is

a nonstarter? Vanessa's advice echoes my own: Don't feel like everything has to happen for you right away, and that you're a failure if it doesn't.

Don't feel like everything has to happen for you right away, and that you're a failure if it doesn't.

She observes: "A lot of that has to do with just the way that the world is now. We're available 24/7, 365 days a year, and are expected to respond rapidly to everything that comes across our path. We internalize that expectation and we decide that it means that if I move fast enough and quick enough, I'll be recognized faster and quicker. And the fastest one wins.

"But that's not the case at all, because what you're losing out on is that time to meditate, that time to step back, to look at what you're doing and see the different steps that you're taking, how they're lining up: Are they lining up in the way that makes sense for you? Or are you just moving so fast that you really don't have time to evaluate?"

If you are thinking of pivoting in your career, it's so important to take the time to dig deep. You've had several years of learning and absorbing—and by the way, that will be the case for the rest of your career—but think about the root of why you are rushing things.

If you are thinking of pivoting in your career, it's so important to take the time to dig deep. You've had several years of learning and absorbing—and by the way, that will be the case

for the rest of your career—but think about the root of why
you are rushing things.

It can be counterproductive. Vanessa says: "That sets us up to feel like failures way too early in our lives. And I guess that's what's different now. Even when my parents were coming along, they were conditioned to not having everything handed to them right away, to things not being readily available, having to strive a bit."

She adds: "We don't talk a lot about striving now. We just talk a lot about achieving. And that's the difference. Maybe we need to set more realistic expectations for ourselves, not to limit our goals, not at all, but to consider that the journey to getting there—and how you feel about it—is just as important as actually getting there."

Starting Over

Dia Simms is another great example of achieving great success by risking a career change—and perhaps having to start over in the process. After college, she worked in the Department of Defense, in advertising sales, and in the pharmaceutical industry before being presented with the opportunity to work for music and business mogul Sean "Diddy" Combs.

She was offered a job as his assistant, and in some ways had to start over. But in that role, she learned to manage large groups of people, learned Combs's business inside and out, and eventually rose through the ranks to become president. This was an opportunity that wouldn't have come up if Simms hadn't followed her gut. She didn't see that opportunity to work as an assistant in her late 20s as a setback. On the contrary, it proved to be an incredible opportunity.

Step back and consider the possibilities for success and growth, instead of wallowing in the pressure to make "the perfect choice."

Simms advises young women along these lines: "Make a decision and make it the right decision." She encourages all women, and young women especially, to take risks: "You'll be surprised at your capabilities."

One of the things she tells women to be wary about is overanalyzing decision-making. As women, we are the worst at managing this; we can actually paralyze ourselves from moving forward!

Step back and consider the possibilities for success and growth, instead of wallowing in the pressure to make "the perfect choice." This will empower and embolden you.

Dia reflects: "I see so many young women executives who spend years in pursuit of the perfect decision. For example, when you're picking an outfit, you have to make a choice. Wear it with confidence. No one knows the outfit you didn't choose. Approach your life and career with the same decisiveness and confidence."

"Most CEO pathways are not linear. Gaining exposure in a broad array of industries enhances your technical leadership skills and your body of relationships."

Take as an example Dia's training in negotiation at the Department of Defense. She had developed skills from her early career in a completely different industry, but ultimately it allowed her to hone skills and tactics that would be invaluable. They were transferable skills. When it came time to negotiate multibillion-dollar contracts at Combs Enterprises, she had a real advantage. If you're feeling stuck, ask yourself: What am I learning right now (even if it's difficult, negative, or less than ideal!) that is building my character to help me get where I want to go?

Carla Harris echoes this point and says you should think of your professional lifetime as a combination of many careers. "You are going to have five to six careers, not jobs, over the course of a thirty-year career."

> ... you should think of your professional lifetime as a combination of many careers. You are going to have five to six careers, not jobs, over the course of a thirty-year career.
> —CARLA HARRIS

She advises young professionals to check in with themselves and assess their goals: "Every five years, they ought to check themselves to see if the job or career they're in is still giving them personal value. Are they still intellectually challenged? Are they making a contribution to the broader world? Are they using that platform to extend into different things? Are they getting appropriately compensated for what they're doing? If that career is still giving them a compelling value proposition, no need to move. If not, it may be time that they leverage the experience into something else. That's when you come across things that you may feel passionate about."

For example, when Carla started as a first-year associate, she wasn't involved in anything philanthropic, which eventually became a big passion of hers.

"Someone I met while I was interviewing somewhere else kept in touch. She exposed me to the Food Bank in New York City. That's when I realized that I had a passion for eradicating hunger. I couldn't figure out how a city as rich as NYC had so many people that were challenged just to eat every day. I began working with the food bank and that was one of my key charities for twenty years. That became a passion.

"Keep yourself open to having new experiences and you'll find as things come up, you'll make time in your calendar. That's about being organized and intentional. There are twenty-four hours in a day; for eight of them hopefully you're sleeping." Carla stresses the need to use the other sixteen hours to do something for you. Nurture a passion or check in with things that make you feel good and that you enjoy.

Before she was made CEO of Vimeo, Anjali Sud had stints in several different companies. "I've done everything from investment banking to working for media companies like Time Warner to a bunch of different things at Amazon; everything from being a toy buyer to marketing diapers online." As you read in earlier chapters, she stressed that careers nowadays are not linear. Building a strong inner compass to guide you is an important part of getting to your next step.

We asked Anjali what she based her decisions on when it came to switching gears or changing jobs in her 20s. "My compass has always been to get out of my comfort zone. In every job I've had, the day I felt like I wasn't learning as much as I did on day one was the day I was ready for change."

And everyone is different, Sud acknowledges: "It all comes down to: What's your motivation?"

What drove her to make decisions in her career was a hunger to learn. "If I was in a job where I felt like I had been drinking from the fire hose, and I was learning and every day was something new, I was really engaged and in it 100 percent. The day I felt like, okay, I figured this out, I would find myself hungry to discover the next thing. That drove me to move around a lot in my career. It also drove me to try different functions. My philosophy has always been that a diversity of experiences makes you a better leader. It makes you a more nimble and effective decision-maker; I was very focused on that.

"Of course, there were many instances where my boss didn't agree with that philosophy, and I respect that. In which case, I just wasn't the right fit for that company. It meant that I should probably look to do something else."

What worked for Anjali was embracing her true self. And that took figuring out. She tried to fit the mold of what she thought was required in several jobs; but ultimately, when she was comfortable enough with her ideas, she spoke up and stood firm, which brought her to where she is now.

"In one of my interviews, they told me they didn't think I had the personality to be an investment banker. There's a perception of investment bankers and their demeanor that maybe I didn't express, but it also wasn't my authentic self."

She had in some ways worked around the unconscious bias of what a woman in finance was supposed to act like. "The way I conducted myself or dressed or how young I looked, my natural communication style, probably didn't align with the traditional perception of 'investment banker.'"

Early in her career, she tried to combat that bias by changing parts of herself to fit in: "I tried to be one of the guys—to dress, or act, or speak in a way that I thought would reflect the more typical stereotypes. For me that didn't prove to be a very effective tactic, because it was ultimately just an act."

She says that what worked for her and proved to be effective was to confront bias with objective measures: "Bias comes from subjectivity, so the more you can just hone in on objective results—like metrics and performance—the more you can combat bias."

Now that she's in her 30s and a CEO, she has a different perspective. "I now believe the only way to shatter stereotypes is to be very transparent and publicly me. That means that I dress the way I want, I communicate in the style that feels natural to me and my personality. I don't shy away from the fact that I'm a woman, and I talk openly and unapologetically about things like my pregnancy, or that time I burst into tears after a meeting.

"Now it's really my responsibility to help break these stereotypes by being real and providing more examples of people who are doing things a little bit differently. My perspective on this has certainly changed. I went through many phases. Initially, I tried to conform. Then I tried to keep things objective, which helped me get to where I am today. Now I feel a responsibility to proactively reduce stereotypes and to do it in as transparent a way as possible."

And in getting to where she is, she's demonstrated an attribute often derided in young people: "I have been accused several times in my career of being too impatient."

Anjali admits that she was aware of this in her career and worried it might work against her: "I have definitely held back at times because I didn't want to come across as too ambitious, or as not playing by the rules. And I've had bosses, including women, tell me I was being too impatient in asking for a bigger role."

But the big aha moment in her career was owning her own impatience: she caught herself embracing it, telling herself, "I am deeply impatient. I am very ambitious."

The fact of the matter is that some people assemble their building blocks quickly: they learn at an accelerated rate and apply the tools we discussed early in this book effectively, early on. And that itch to get ahead doesn't stem from a dismissal of the hard tasks in front of them. For people like Anjali, it was about challenging herself, and always taking advantage of new opportunities to learn and grow.

She observes: "If I'm really good at my job, I want to keep that learning curve steep. Just the simple of act of admitting that to myself and saying it out loud, 'Anjali, you are deeply impatient and very ambitious' allowed me to own it. This is who I am. I am this person. I can either treat it as a flaw or I can view it as a strength."

That realization propelled her to look for roles and companies she thought would appreciate her style. It helped her drive her inner compass on what to do next. She focused on companies and people that exuded who she was as a learning professional: "It's one of the reasons I came to Vimeo, whose parent company is chaired by Barry Diller. He has been public about promoting hungry and inexperienced leaders into big roles—throwing them into the deep end of the pool and seeing if they can swim. That sort of trial-by-fire approach, which I'd read about, was one of the reasons I came here.

"I left Amazon to come to Vimeo by recognizing that this is who I am. I was going to own it, which helped me decide which company was right for the next stage of my career. It ended up being the right move."

She finds that her early worry about coming off as too ambitious is a common feeling for other young women; and she encourages them to embrace it: "If you own your ambition, you can turn that into a strength. I did my research. In the interview process and when making the ultimate decision to join Vimeo, I was very conscious of it. I explicitly looked for a company I thought would be a good fit for my ambition."

> **If you own your ambition, you can turn that into a strength.**
> —ANJALI SUD

In your first few years in the workplace, go for it—take some risks and experiment with different career decisions. At this point in your career, you should be used to change. Look for it all around you. Talk all the time to the people you work with and to people you meet when you're out socializing. Learn about different careers and opportunities, and don't be afraid to take a chance or two. You have time to really explore.

Use stories like Anjali's as an inspiration and focus on building your skills for your own success. If you do get that success earlier, great! Some young people know exactly what they want and have laser vision on how to get there. But if not, do not get discouraged; don't second-guess your choices as you navigate through the early part of your career.

Just because you are ambitious and impatient doesn't mean your dream job will manifest itself overnight. Stop comparing yourself. Take your time to learn with each career move and allow each role to help grow your confidence the way Anjali did. It helped her grow into her own skin. And when she was ready both professionally and personally, the job that allowed her to be her authentic self and to work on her skill set was right there. Good things come when you embrace challenges and opportunities to learn.

Work on your skill set: it will pay off.

Tips on Pivoting

Maybe you're thinking after reading this, "It's really time to start looking elsewhere." There are a few more things to consider.

Take this time to acknowledge what doesn't work at your current job so you don't re-create it elsewhere. If you're going to exit, Liz Bentley advises, "Don't leave until you've got something good to leverage.... Make sure you're going for something better, or at least equal, that's going to make sense, and make sure you're going for a culture that works for you."

But be cautious of going into a culture that stops challenging you. Liz notes that some of her clients will go for cultures that "make sense for them," but they're not going to be happy going to work every day, because they're no longer growing, and eventually their careers get marginalized: "I almost find that people are way too willing to jump instead of willing to grow—that jumping prevents their growth, and that's really dangerous."

If you are serious about moving to another company or perhaps to another industry entirely, carefully consider how you are going to do that.

Even meeting someone just for information with the purpose of perhaps moving elsewhere can backfire if you don't do it discreetly, if it's in your same line of work.

But if you are thinking about changing industries in general, and there is little probability that it will get back to your boss or company, executive coach Liz Bentley says that's fair game: "A lot of bosses look at your LinkedIn profile, so they can tell if they think you're shopping. You need to very careful about looking for a new job while you're in your current one."

That's not to say you shouldn't set up any informationals: the key is to do them confidentially, Bentley says. "Start with a conversation with someone you feel you know well enough and say, 'I'm thinking about leaving, but I just want to hear how it's going in your organization. And I don't want this getting back to anyone in my company because I'm not necessarily leaving. I just want to understand how it's going.'

"You have to work with people you trust first and dip your toe very lightly in the water before you go too deep, and not be mindless, like 'Oh, we just went for coffee, it's no big deal'— because if someone sees you going for coffee, they're going to be suspicious that you're leaving."

You don't want to do anything that exacerbates the stereotypes of young professionals being disloyal or serial job-hoppers.

Bentley also recommends considering that it might be easier to get promoted where you are than to go elsewhere: "I always say work both sides of the fence: work internally where you are and work externally for the next thing. But I think it's always easier to get promoted internally. And everyone thinks that the grass is greener somewhere else.

"If you move up internally, it shows that you're good at what you're doing, you're being appreciated. You want to be moving up continually inside your own job. Whether that's just getting more responsibility or it's getting a new title. And that's all on you. If you're doing a really good job, they're going to give you more responsibility. It's just the way it is. If they're not giving you more responsibilities, it's because you're not doing a really good job. Additionally, internal moves are usually promotions at the beginning of your career, whereas external moves might be lateral. It can be hard to get promoted in a move until you are further up the food chain."

That's when taking a step back and digging deep into the root of your dissatisfaction is essential.

CHAPTER NINE

GOING OUT ON YOUR OWN

It took years for me to feel comfortable captaining my own ship. I kept my head down, did the work, and stayed grateful for my job. Sure, I wasn't making the rules; but things were stable. It wasn't until after the success of my first book, *Knowing Your Value: Women, Money, and Getting What You're Worth*, that I realized I could build something from the ground up. It took me decades to realize that I might have a message worth sharing with other women.

Young women today have a fire in their bellies to create change and dream big. This might involve working for themselves in ways earlier generations couldn't have imagined.

Instead of succumbing to old ways of doing things, young women recognize the value of changing the system—of being creative disrupters. Cindi Leive, who managed and hired hundreds of young women through her time at Condé Nast, says: "Their attitude is 'This company needs to meet me on my terms; otherwise I'm going to go out and start my own thing.'"

But owning your own business and branching out on your own isn't for everyone. It takes a lot of nerve to become an entrepreneur, even in this age of seemingly overnight success hyped by social media. And it's A LOT of work—not always glamorous. But there are young women who've done the traditional 9-to-5 job, or have navigated the corporate world, and wake up one day and realize: "Great! I've learned a lot of really great skills, but I want to move on to my own project."

Yes, it's a big leap! But the women I highlight below show how they did it—not just by owning their brands, but also by strategically building them into robust businesses.

Building a Business from Your Brand

Even if you are still trying to figure out what your brand is, you can start building it by determining the pillars that are important to you. Here are some examples of how a few successful women built and grew their personal and professional brands to the point that they own their destiny—that is, their own company.

Martha Stewart, who has built a globally recognized brand and is a household name, encourages millennials to build their professional brands around accuracy and authenticity: "Work hard to develop an in-depth knowledge of your subject matter. You just can't fake it; people realize you're not authentic when they delve deep into your subject." Not only do you need an authentic message: you also have to be accurate in its execution.

Martha uses the example of baking a cake: "When we publish a cake recipe, for example, we start by researching and developing the recipe, and then we test it repeatedly to make sure it's clear, works accurately, and results in a delicious cake. If your recipe is not well-written and in-depth, forget it! Your readers and customers will not come back to you. They want accuracy and they want authenticity. Building a brand requires that."

Fashion designer Tory Burch agrees that a successful brand should be grounded in authenticity. She also stresses "the need for something unique that will make your brand stand out. It's not necessarily about what you know; it's about learning and intellectual curiosity, being unique and having a vision—a unique point of view.

"I was just doing it [creating her own brand], but it wasn't like I said, 'I want to be an entrepreneur.' I was actually finding my passion before I knew that I'd turned into an entrepreneur."

Her advice to young women: "In order to be an entrepreneur, you have to realize what your passion is. It can't just be a blanket 'I want to be an entrepreneur,' because you become entrepreneurial and act entrepreneurial in every job you do. To start up a business, you need an authentic idea. It has to be real and it has to answer a need if it is going to be successful."

In other words, Tory was doing what she loved, and it grew beyond her personal brand organically to become a real business.

Sarah Jessica Parker is an Emmy-nominated actress who has created an entire new brand for herself outside of acting, not to mention her credits as producer, director, and even as a book publisher. Being the CEO and brand strategist of her own line of shoes, SJP Collection, she knows a thing or two about curating an amazing brand and reinventing herself creatively.

Taking charge of your own professional optics takes time and experience. What you show the world about your brand will open doors to new opportunities and avenues for success that will help your professional growth. Here are a few things to learn from SJP's playbook on building a sustainable and successful brand.

Find a Mentor to Help with Your Messaging and Delivery

For the launch of SJP Collection, Sarah Jessica partnered with the best in the business when it comes to shoes: George Malkemus, CEO of Manolo Blahnik, a veteran in footwear fashion for more than forty years.

Why? She explains, "I can defer to him for very good counsel and growth."

By partnering with one of the best in the business, Sarah Jessica was able to leverage her skills and bring her people-savvy to really grow and nurture the business.

Whether you are at the beginning of your career or reinventing it by taking a different path, expanding your professional brand will be elevated if you can find a mentor or sponsor to bring the skills you've honed to a new level. By enlisting an expert to expand your experiences, you can grow your professional brand and amplify the scope of influence your brand can have.

> Finding the right mentor was a consistent theme that we heard in focus groups we conducted with Harvard researchers to prepare for this book. Especially among members of Gen Z we heard that finding a mentor who listens to them and helps

them chart their unique path, which may be different than the mentor's path, was sometimes difficult, but the most rewarding. "Good mentors don't say, 'You'll do great,' they say, 'You should be working more on this,'" they told John Della Volpe, who moderated these discussions.

You Will Always Be Building Your Brand

Whether you are working to build a business or creating your professional brand, the same rules apply. You will always be adding, adjusting, editing, and evolving your brand, the same way you update your résumé as new opportunities open up.

Take, for example, the fashion industry: if you don't constantly evolve and find ways to reinvent trends, you won't succeed in the long run. Some of the smartest and most hardworking women I know in the fashion industry, like Michelle Smith from Milly, Rebecca Minkoff, and especially Sarah Jessica Parker, have had to be incredibly nimble to keep their brands up to speed with the pulse of fashion and its audience.

Even if it might seem that some of my fashion designer friends have made it, they will tell you that it's a never-ending process of maintenance to build a brand, because you will always be working at it. Having that mentality will help inform decisions. If you think of yourself as a brand, the choices you make become part of your trajectory—your successes and even your failures. Sometimes you learn and evolve the most from failures that make you pick yourself up. The key is to create the story line that turns each choice into part of your professional story.

Sarah Jessica Parker observes: "You don't stop working. Even the established fashion houses have to keep finding new ways to grow. A business isn't a stagnant entity with a beginning and an end. A business requires 100 percent of your time and dedication and talent and effort. It's not unlike producing a television series or being a parent in some ways. It's an ongoing, ever-evolving experience, and my philosophy about work is that it deserves all of me.

> A business isn't a stagnant entity with a beginning and an end. A business requires 100 percent of your time and dedication and talent and effort.
> —SARAH JESSICA PARKER

"I'm not somebody who has licensing arrangements. I don't just put my name on something and people come to me with a short list and I say 'yes' and 'no.' I'm part of every sales appointment I run with George, every sample that comes in. I'm in every design meeting, and every conversation about marketing or promotion or PR or press, all done with a small team."

Sarah Jessica explains that she spends an enormous amount of time and attention on her shoe line, and constantly finds ways to uphold the brand based on "quality, price point, and its relevance in [consumers'] lives."

She is always looking for ways to keep those elements in balance.

Grow Your Brand Strategically by Knowing Your Audience

For Parker, branching out from TV to retail with her shoe line took daily work as well as knowing her audience and customers at the other side of that messaging.

"The brand is sort of my answer to this relationship I was given an opportunity to cultivate with a gang of ten million women who watched a show I was on for a long time," she says, referencing the huge hit *Sex and the City*.

She adds: "I've been fortunate enough to continue the conversation. My customers are a very big part of the inspiration and the thinking behind the shoes and the bags and the dresses. And it's why I work so hard. I go to Bloomingdale's four or five times a year simply to work on the floor and sell shoes and listen to the customers. No hair and makeup and press, just me traveling from store to store."

Find Brand Inspiration

It always helps to construct your brand by seeing how others have done it. Whom do you admire? What can you learn from them about delivery? What has worked for them?

For Sarah Jessica Parker, that inspiration came from Laura Mercier. Sarah Jessica says: "A big part of my business was built on the way Laura Mercier built her brand. Twenty-five years ago, she started her cosmetics line, her color line, and she had no marketing dollars or PR dollars; I didn't, either.

"She just went from store to store, talked to customers, worked on their faces, heard what they needed, heard what they wanted, heard what worked and didn't. In my case it's size, it's the feel of the shoe, it's what my customers require: what they need versus what they want. It's been enormously beneficial for us to have those conversations."

Sarah Jessica has built a great brand with her acting and entertainment career, but she has also learned to manage and grow it because she has showed a great ability to pound the pavement—to get out there and listen to people. She has input with every detail of the brand she has built, while also leveraging her past careers.

Branching Out

Carly Zakin and Danielle Weisberg, founders of the popular daily email newsletter theSkimm, gradually moved into the role of entrepreneurs after they both began at NBC in entry-level roles at NBC News and CNBC. They were able to make extensions of their brand into a business based on what they learned from their first few years in the corporate world.

They both agree about the value of working first in a big company.

Carly says: "I didn't leave and start theSkimm because I was done with corporate America; I actually loved working at a big company."

Aside from what she and her partner, Danielle, learned working alongside top-notch journalists, they also value knowing how to work in a professional environment: how to have managers, how to be around people you're intimidated by—and how not to be intimidated by them. So how did Carly get noticed in a large and competitive work environment?

"Early on, someone told me—and they were very much joking—'You're kind of like Forrest Gump. You just keep showing up.'"

She took it as a bit of a dig, because she considers herself a little shy: "I'm naturally not an extrovert. It's not easy for me to go into a big environment and be the loud one, or to make myself known. But I figured out how to network, find anchors in different rooms I wanted to be in, to be in front of the leadership and the executives.

"Even if it was just saying that I'd met them once, I had their email address and I'd be able to follow up: I was able to build a network that way. When I think back to those earliest days, people probably had no idea what my name was: I was just that girl who kept waving at them or writing them a congratulatory note that they probably didn't respond to. But it developed into a professional working relationship."

Since working for a large corporation and developing their professional brand from working for someone else to working for themselves, their brand today is "never stop."

That could be the motto of so many self-starters: the work doesn't end at 5 p.m. or even 7 p.m. or much later.

Danielle Weisberg admits that in her early days at NBC News, she was a bit of a "polite stalker." She tried to identify people in positions to hire and to make change—not necessarily top executives: "I looked at the people whose career I wanted, and who had started off like me. I would try to get coffee with them, and then follow up."

Sometimes her hustle went too far: "I remember an email from someone I had emailed five times in a row; I really wanted to be on his show. He said, 'There's a difference between being aggressive and taking it too far.'"

Though she may have straddled that line in the company, in starting her own with Carly, Danielle has come to value "that spirit of fearlessness, because we really focus on hustle. I think reaching out, asking questions, networking—those are the things that came intuitively to us, and that was what got the company off the ground in those early years."

She emphasizes that the decision to start your own enterprise is a very personal one: "There's no magical moment."

It's always going to be a major leap of faith to invest your own money, or that of family and friends to start. The two started theSkimm with credit card debt, which, as Carly points out, "kept us motivated. We're really grateful that our families couldn't support us." But she and Danielle didn't necessarily see leaving NBC as an audacious gamble.

Danielle explains: "Given the rapid way media is changing, and the consolidation in the business, in retrospect, I think we made a safer choice by deciding to own our own destiny. That was something we felt when we decided to quit our jobs with no money and start something from our couch, but couldn't really articulate until now, six years in."

Given the rapid way media is changing, and the consolidation in
the business, in retrospect, I think we made a safer choice by
deciding to own our own destiny.
—DANIELLE WEISBERG

Putting it into perspective, they were both 25 when they started
theSkimm. And as she puts it: "We weren't making much money
to begin with—so the stakes were low enough that we knew it
would never get easier. This was the least scary it would ever be.

"That's a decision you have to make for yourself, but I would
encourage people to define security in different ways—especially
in this environment, where we don't know what jobs are going
to look like five, ten, or twenty years from now."

Today theSkimm has more than 7 million readers, employs
some 75 people, and just raised $12 million in funding. Its
reported valuation is around $100 million dollars. The goal for
the two highly successful young hustlers?

As Carly puts it: "To be the most important brand for a
generation of female millennials. And we believe that we can be
that and that we are that, because of what our mission is: we
make it easier to live a smarter life."

Keep in mind—when you have a big vision and ask for other
people's opinions, take them with a grain of salt. There is never
a shortage of naysayers who might derail you for your big idea.
Carly looks back on a conversation she once had with someone
she respected highly, who told her that instead of starting her
own company, she should focus on having a personal life: "That
broke my heart, because I wasn't saying I was choosing work over

being a person or having a family or a relationship or children one day. She basically told me to slow down. And I think that that is the worst thing that you can ever say to someone who has a vision, because that's just gonna make them work harder.

"While it was the most painful advice to hear, it was probably the best thing for me to hear, because I just wanted to work really hard to prove her wrong." And that's exactly what she did.

While I highly recommend that you expand your network and listen to those who want to help you navigate the potential pitfalls, always remember to follow your own intuition. Being able to listen critically is key; take what helps you grow and put aside the rest.

Jane Park didn't become a business owner right out of the gate: she came to entrepreneurship after a series of career changes.

In an earlier chapter, we looked at her decision to ditch a safe legal career. By the time Jane started Julep Beauty when she was 33, she was able to draw on experiences working as a management consultant, and at Starbucks: "One of the most helpful things I did was read Howard Schultz's book *Pour Your Heart into It: How Starbucks Built a Company One Cup at a Time*.

"What's true in any part of your career is how lonely you can feel; there's no one else who has done it quite like you. I didn't know any other Korean immigrant mom with two kids who was trying to start a business.

"This is another myth that women often fall victim to: you're looking for the person with your exact situation to light the way for you. And truth is, often that person doesn't exist; you need to cobble together lessons from different people around you."

This strikes me as another version of my "find a side door" advice from earlier in this book: there is no owner's manual or Holy Grail for a job hunt or a start-up. It's all about exposing yourself to as many learning experiences as possible, and building on the knowledge gained, including a key one: how to learn from failure.

Jane Park says that one of the main things she learned from Howard Schultz was how to navigate the many bumps in the road new business owners will encounter before hitting on the right path forward.

It's all about exposing yourself to as many learning experiences as possible, and building on the knowledge gained, including a key one: how to learn from failure.

She admires the straight talk in his book: "A lot of times male entrepreneurs don't share honestly what it's like to build a company. I think Howard was one of the few who talked about all the 'nos' he got at first. If you talk to the Silicon Valley bros, you know they're always killing it.

"It was super helpful when Howard talked about the 'nos,' to make the challenges part of the journey. I think another myth we fall victim to is that things just seem easy: if you know you're doing your best, it should all be working. It shouldn't be so challenging and hard. One of the biggest lessons I'd love to share with women is that it's all hard—and it gets harder."

It's easier to face rejection, says Park, if you see it as part of the process: "Then you know that it isn't outside the ordinary experience—that you are not particularly a loser having to navigate an experience everybody has gone through. That makes rejection a heightening experience that doesn't feel so lonely. If you take every 'no' as a sign that you shouldn't be doing this, it's hard to get anywhere."

Park's take is that women can "grow their confidence" by putting themselves in more risk-taking situations: "It's not like you're born with X amount of confidence and you live your life with it. It's like a muscle—you can grow it. The way you exercise it is to put yourself in situations where you take risks."

One of the biggest risks of starting a new business is of course financing it. One of the main things that can kill a new company is running out of capital.

As Jane puts it: "Almost everything else is survivable. The search for capital is such a critical one for new companies. It is horrifying that so many venture capital companies are not anywhere close to gender parity. The funding for women-headed start-ups is anywhere from 2 to 9 percent—in single digits, which is not anywhere the workforce is.

"But you know, everything is a challenge, and everything is new when starting a company. Almost every single day you're doing hundreds of things you've never done before."

Park got more comfortable with being uncomfortable—that is, moving out of her personal comfort zone, in an early job as a strategy consultant at the Boston Consulting Group: "I worked in pharmaceuticals and automotive windshield wipers, lots of different areas where I had no expertise.

"There is a metric that BCG uses in their review process

which I have always loved, called the 'tolerance for ambiguity.' It asks, do you freak out when you're in a situation where there are lots of unknowns, or do you dive in and do whatever you can to get to the best answer as quickly as possible? In those situations, there is no time for niceties."

Sounds like ideal training to start your own business!

Park adds a key point that may not be visible yet to millennial entrepreneurs: "The more risks you take, the more mistakes you're going to make."

She points out that when she worked for a large organization, she made perhaps one big decision a year, moving things along in the business. When she made so few consequential decisions, she also made fewer mistakes.

In contrast, she observes: "As an entrepreneur, you're making hundreds of decisions a day. They might all be smaller: you know, where does the light switch go? How much are you going to pay this person versus that person? But you've got to make all the calls. You're learning along the way.

"You can spend all your time beating yourself up over things you wish you'd done better. It's important to realize you can't have that moment over again, but you can do it differently the next time with the next person. Sometimes you get a do-over with the same person.

"Beating yourself up doesn't help anybody. You have to say, 'This is what I'm going to do the next time.' Mistakes don't turn themselves into lessons by themselves: you have to work at it."

This is so key for women: business is NOT PERSONAL.

You need to own your mistakes, as much if not more than you own your successes. It's the only way forward—not an easy task. In fact, there isn't really an easy path.

Looking back, says Jane Park, "I wish someone had told me how hard it was going to be—not to discourage me from entrepreneurship, but the opposite: to prepare me, so that when I was facing difficulties, I wouldn't feel like it was something I was doing wrong—that it was my fault."

This is so key for women: business is NOT PERSONAL.

Then there are the clear rewards of seeing your vision realized and helping to change people's lives in the process. When people ask Jane Park why she started Julep, she answers this way: "It's always been about empowering women. I think a lot of my professors in the women's studies classes I took, and the gender equality classes I took in law school, would have been surprised that I started a beauty company."

For her, it was about changing the conversation.

"When we were starting Julep ten years ago, there was no Dove campaign, there was no idea of beauty being about fun, about me—it was more about striving for a perfect, unattainable idea of beauty. We were starting with physical nail parlors. Most women who worked in that business—and it's all women—didn't have access to health care benefits and were breathing in toxic fumes. I wanted to change that.

"What do you think happens when you go to a nail salon and you pay ten dollars for a manicure? That woman serving you is not getting health care, and she's breathing in toxic fumes. Many women I know, who are all about empowering other women and environmental justice, and eat organic everything, have a little bubble around themselves when they walk into a discount nail salon."

Ouch! I know these women. And I bet you do, too.

Jane Park adds: "From day one, we trained people, and gave them access to health care benefits. All the women who work for us talk about that as the number one thing. They're almost all single moms, and they would have no access to health care in the whole industry they work in, except for Julep.

"I think that if you have a true north that you care about, it comes out in all the things that you do. There were a lot of different businesses I could have started. In some ways, you don't have to wait for the perfect thing. You have so much more impact in the daily things that you do, and the decisions you make around the workforce that you're hiring, or the workplace you're engaging in. I think that's as important as the idea."

For some young women, becoming an entrepreneur comes naturally. Katlyn Grasso, the 25-year-old founder and CEO of the start-up GenHERation®, says she was always inclined to it: "My dad would tell me when I was growing up, 'It's not always the school that makes the person, it's the person who makes the school.' I don't think going to business school and being in Accounting 101 taught me how to be an entrepreneur. Going to a place where people were really open about sharing their success, and showing how people make things happen, is what made me a successful entrepreneur."

Her can-do attitude dictates that whether you live in a small town or a metropolis like New York, "your job is to go out there as an entrepreneur and collect as much information as possible. There are always opportunities to grow and hone your skills, whether you're meeting someone for coffee and asking them about their job or taking a class. It doesn't necessarily involve writing a business plan or doing something you think is exactly relatable to what you're doing then."

What she said resonated with me; when I started my Know Your Value business partnership with NBCUniversal, I had never created a business plan, P&L, or marketing plan before. But I knew smart women and where to find them. I gathered up the many positive connections I had made over the years and asked them questions. I built a team out of women I already trusted who helped me fill in the gaps.

I started to develop what Grasso calls the "entrepreneurship muscle that you have to flex. When you're building muscle, you need to do it every day until you almost get muscle memory. For instance, when I think about the key skills entrepreneurs need, they're problem-solving; being able to think on your feet; and being able to connect people and ideas. You don't need to take entrepreneurship classes or go to business school to implement them.

"Experience can come from any aspect of your life. Did you sell Girl Scout cookies when you were 10 years old? You can apply the skills you learned then to fundraising and managing a team."

As you can tell by her tone, Grasso combines entrepreneurial energy with a core practicality. She had a fateful run-in with the woman who would award her with her first grant, in the ladies' room of all places, at the Wharton School. At the time, she'd been looking for a small grant of $1,500 to study girls' leadership development; nobody was coming through.

While washing her hands, Grasso said to the woman at the next sink: "What do you do here?"

The answer? "Actually, I run the Wharton Social Impact Initiative. I'm here conducting interviews to fund summer research grants."

Grasso's grant went through right there at the sink—all stemming from her simple outreach.

Not everyone will be so lucky, or as well-placed as a student at a top school like Wharton. But Grasso's point is that by always getting out and observing and asking questions, you are honing skills that will serve you in unexpected ways. And you can start small.

You can build crucial muscle memory in different ways.

After Grasso received the inaugural $150,000 President's Engagement Prize from Penn President Dr. Amy Gutmann, to develop a social business with the potential to change the world, she focused her efforts on the national expansion of her company. Katlyn believes that it is important to leverage the power of your community to advance your entrepreneurial goals, whether it's through alumni groups, professional organizations, your colleagues at work, or growing your leadership skills by "volunteering to serve on alumni boards," among other things.

In 2016, Katlyn launched a program called GenHERation Discovery Days, a cross-country bus tour that takes girls to visit the most innovative companies in America. At various corporate headquarters the girls and executives at the companies make a one-on-one connection. Some of the participants had started getting back to her with news like, "Hey, I got a job with this company because I went on Discovery Days."

Grasso observes: "That really led us to change our whole business model to become a marketplace where young women and companies connect. I realized that we could provide services that allow companies to engage with our audience in meaningful ways."

She doubts that she ever would have included this model in a business plan for her company five years before that, because she wouldn't have had this direct feedback, to know what was genuinely needed: "Hearing from the girls and the companies shaped and pivoted my whole model right there. You have to be very agile, and you can't always ask people what they think you should do because a lot of people will tell you, 'Oh, go talk to experts,' which is great. Everybody has their own ideas, but if you listen to everybody, you will never get anything done."

"I think the main people you need to talk to are your end users, asking, 'What do you need from me?' and being open to change. That was something that took me a bit longer to learn. I included specific details in my application for the prize based on where I thought we were going; but then I had to revise those plans and do something else that better served our members."

She began building her team with free interns, and initially worked out of her apartment. She advises: "When you're starting a business, you should be as lean as possible. I heard an entrepreneur speak who said, 'People would always come to me and ask, How big are you?' Unless they had 100 employees, they thought they were small. But it's not quantity of employees that matters, it's the quality. You can have five people who are just as effective as fifty; don't feel like you have to be flashy just because that's what the cover of a business magazine tells you to do."

Katlyn Grasso is all about the art of the possible and listening to your prospective customers.

In terms of making key connections, she has a suggestion for young women thinking about becoming entrepreneurs: "A long time ago, someone told me that to get 'important or influential people' to talk to you, start a blog. Get a simple WordPress account and say, 'I'm going to try to build expertise around, let's say, scaling a business.' Then reach out to ten successful people who have scaled a business and interview them for your site.

"That's ten people you know sharing their knowledge. Everybody loves to talk about their professional journey and to share their story."

This is the kind of networking 2.0 that's a millennial specialty. Lifestyle blogger Kat Tanita took full advantage of this digital nativism to grow her blog, *With Love From Kat*. She has upward of 380,000 Instagram followers and now works for herself.

A native of Arizona, Tanita was on her own financially from an early age. At 15, she got her first job at a clothing boutique, where she learned about customer service, sales, and presentation. Her passion was always fashion and design.

In college, she majored in interior design and held three unpaid internships at different-size interior design firms, where she could see firsthand how the business worked: "I soon realized while I loved décor, I didn't want to actually become an interior designer."

She graduated a semester early, even while working full-time as a nanny and taking online and night courses. Tanita paid for college herself, the way my associate Daniela did. These are truly motivated young women!

One day Tanita started to investigate blogs to stay up to date in the design field: "That very night I Googled how to start a blog, bought my domain, and came up with the name 'With Love From Kat.'"

At first, she posted pictures of interiors that inspired her: "One of my first posts was about the Avalon Hotel in Beverly Hills, designed by Kelly Wearstler, my interior design idol. It was really just a fun creative outlet, and at the time my mom and sister were the only people reading it."

Soon she was posting every single day: "I always had something new to talk about and share. And it became, literally, my obsession and my hobby."

Just three days after she relocated to New York City, she got a job handling social media for a small fine jewelry company in the heart of the Garment District: "I took the commuter bus in every morning; it was the time of my life."

Though she'd moved to the city worried that she wouldn't survive, her attitude was: "When you're young, you are kind of fearless. I was willing to do whatever it took to survive. I think that has really helped me in my career in that I'm willing to roll up my sleeves and literally do whatever it takes."

She became more and more interested in fashion as she began

to be exposed to high-end designers through her new job. Soon she started talking about some of her favorites on her blog, and posting pictures taken by her boyfriend of what she wore to work and to Central Park on weekends: "I started sharing my tips on favorite restaurants, favorite clothing items. It just naturally evolved into a fashion blog."

> When you're young, you are kind of fearless. I was willing to do whatever it took to survive. I think that has really helped me in my career in that I'm willing to roll up my sleeves and literally do whatever it takes.
>
> —KAT TANITA

Meanwhile, at her job she was learning how to run a company: "I did everything, because it was such a small team. I was doing sales, trunk shows, customer service, invoicing and accounting, negotiating with vendors, inventory, strategy, marketing, design, running all the social media accounts.

"This was eight years ago, so social media was still very new. I was learning as I went, and luckily my boss was okay with that. And the reason I got the job was because of my blog—this hobby of mine, which I'd only had for six months; but I put it on my résumé."

She said something along the lines of: "I write this little blog, and it's about fashion and décor, and I just have a passion for these things."

Tanita almost didn't mention the blog, but in the end, she thought that it might be a good idea to show the boss "a little bit more of a personal piece, and that's what stuck out."

At the jewelry company, Tanita learned how to use MailChimp for email marketing, Dropbox for storing and sharing files, and QuickBooks. She learned how to "negotiate with men in the Diamond District for stones—I learned about profits, margins, losses, and logistics planning. All these things I didn't know how to do and didn't go to college for."

Looking back, Kat Tanita says: "I didn't realize it at the time, but I was learning how to run a business in that job. I learned really quickly from start to finish what it takes, and I think that's what gave me the confidence to start my own."

Another key lesson for young job seekers: take advantage of serendipity. And be open to jobs in fields you never considered in your undergraduate education. If you put yourself out there, you never know where the world might take you.

After a year and a half at the jewelry company, Kat quit. When she failed to get a high-profile public relations job, she decided to take advantage of what she knew best: at age 23, she started a social media business.

With barely enough money to eat and her back to the wall, she forged ahead and figured out the logistics of how to start and run a business. Suddenly she found herself in the right place at the right time, as Pinterest was founded, and social media was starting to build exponentially. Booking a big campaign with Nordstrom was the confidence boost she needed to phase out her social media clients.

She notes some of the challenges she faced being in on the ground floor of the social media explosion: "Being in the fore-front of the blogging industry in New York City, I had a hard time being taken seriously. I got to work with incredible big brands when I was young, but it was tricky because I think people didn't understand the power of marketing and social media. They wanted to pay me like $100 to do a huge campaign.

"I didn't really understand photo usage rights or contracts. It was uncharted waters. There weren't really best practices on how to communicate or treat bloggers and companies. I tried to use my professional experience. I was so grateful to have had a foundation in how to negotiate, to invoice, to draw up contracts, and learn about the value of things. I learned how to be professional. Those things really helped me."

Notice the pattern here: she took advantage of every opportunity along the way to supplement her skill set and didn't hesitate to try new challenges. Yet she was always guided by core enthusiasms in fashion and design: this is the more practical way to "follow your passion."

She hasn't regretted going out on her own: "Having my own business is incredible, so empowering. Something I've wanted since I was 9 years old. Of course, there are roadblocks and challenges."

Since she always worked for small companies, she never learned to manage people or how to be a good boss: "I think there's an art to managing people. I give anyone who is a manager a lot of credit. I found it tricky to hire assistants or anyone creative, or to hire people older than me.

"It's hard to manage different personalities, keep them on track, keep them focused. And to find trustworthy people. At that point, I didn't really know to train them properly or give them the guidance they needed."

Facing the challenges of being a young female entrepreneur trying to be taken seriously in places like New York City or L.A., Tanita advises: "It's important to set a foundation and code of conduct for yourself and anyone who's going to join your team. Even if it's a small idea and casual in the beginning. Treat it like a business and lay that foundation. Keep yourself accountable and anyone who's working for you, whether part-time or freelancer, accountable.

"Being too nice has gotten me in trouble and taken advantage of, so having that firm groundwork and setting the tone is important. As women, we apologize for being firm and shy away from being direct. I wish I had known that it's okay to stand my ground and speak up for myself."

Kat adds advice we've already heard both from my associate Daniela and from experienced managers like Cindi Leive: "Remember that the intern you meet may become the president or VP one day, and it's a very small world.

"Never underestimate the power of networking. Develop a firm handshake, a great follow-up email, a beautiful business card. Go to events, meet with people face to face—that has been key for me.

"And absolutely listen to your gut; don't do what everyone else is doing. I'm always learning, growing, and making mistakes every day. Do something you're passionate about, not because it's trendy."

One of the recurring themes in these entrepreneurial stories is the importance of drive. And it's no accident that the children of immigrants, such as my *Morning Joe* associate Daniela, or

Jane Park, or my sister-in-law Natalia Brzezinski, who started
the tech conference Brilliant Minds, are such strong self-starters:
for them it was sink or swim. The daughter of immigrants from
Poland and the Ukraine, Natalia grew up in Chicago, in a tough
neighborhood: "When I was little my parents used to tell me
they came to this country for me; I better be the best damn thing
out there, or I'm a failure.

"I certainly had a borderline traumatic upbringing, but at
the same time I was imbued with a certain drive and grit and
dedication—a very entrepreneurial mentality, and a very flexible
one. If you can transform all the time, you can handle a lot.
It really taught me how to grow symbolically—literally and
figuratively—to speak different languages. I was able to speak
to older generations, younger generations, translate social and
cultural norms across different groups.

"No one ever helped me with my homework, because they
didn't speak English; and no complaining was allowed. I remember very vividly that I would ask, 'Can't you help me with my
college applications? Can't you help me get an internship?'

"My mom would say, 'You know, if you don't like the house
you were given, build your own.'

"I hated it then but now, you know, that is so me. The front
door has never been open for me, so I've been the one digging a
tunnel under the house with my fingernails until I get in."

Natalia feels that in some ways, she was raised like a son,
"because there was a lot put on me. But at the same time, I felt I
could do it. I have a lot of weaknesses, but I don't have a fear to
try things. Failure was common for me; I saw my parents fail all

the time. My dad was losing jobs constantly when I was young. I very much grew up in a house where the struggle was normal, and so was getting over the struggle."

She was a self-starter from a very young age!

Natalia, who is married to my brother Mark, is a millennial who has always leveraged her professional aspirations and her professional brand in a way I didn't immediately understand. And she found great success doing it.

Let me explain.

During the second term of the Obama Administration, my brother Mark was appointed the U.S. ambassador to Sweden. Natalia, who was in her mid-20s at the time, had a big role in representing the United Stated in Sweden as wife of the ambassador.

Taking advantage of the big residence of the embassy they lived in, she brought together people of all backgrounds to meet and mingle—royal families, entrepreneurs, celebrities, you name it. In quintessentially millennial mode, she thought: we need to share this.

She did a lot of outreach on social media: "As a digital native I brought my skills into networking in Sweden. Being in a role like that in an embassy, people might be afraid to approach me; but they'd send me a message on Facebook, and I always responded. And if people saw on there that I was visiting a tech university or a tech start-up, people would say, let's invite her to our start-up."

She communicated with people, like royal family members who usually have handlers and have a strict communication protocol, by reaching out to them through texts and calls. She didn't take the usual route of using official middlemen.

She ruffled a lot of feathers, especially among older people. The way she did it was very millennial—very transparent and open. From the start, she didn't really follow protocols the way they had been followed before.

Natalia blogged, was active on Instagram, and even had her own podcast. Diplomatic spouses didn't do that back in the day. Natalia was constantly taking pictures with everyone who was coming through the embassy, posting pictures of high-profile people who had stopped for a lunch or meetings at the estate.

Frankly, at the time, I thought she was oversharing. Some of the things that she posted on social media were out there. She was always taking selfies with whoever stopped by to visit. I thought it was a little too much, and I let her know it.

I would call her in Sweden and say, "Natalia, what are you doing? You need to stop sharing everything online!" And I wasn't the only one. It was expected that diplomatic families would do things a certain way, and Natalia the millennial wasn't following those rules.

She pushed the envelope, but the way Natalia brought people together was intentional, strategic, and goal-oriented—and that's why it was effective. It wasn't self-promotion. She was using technology and social media to connect, but she was also using face-to-face engagement to make meaningful relationships with people. It was a hybrid of both, not one or the other.

Everything was done with openness and transparency. She leveraged her platform at the embassy and brought together people who rarely would be seen in the same room and had open conversations on the future of technology, innovation, and politics. It was an open forum of diversity and creativity. Young technology entrepreneurs, who didn't engage with politicians at the time, were now stopping by the embassy. Natalia found herself bringing politics and technology into the same room.

She explains: "In Sweden, politicians and businesspeople did not meet a lot. Young tech people stayed far the hell away from politicians. There was a total line. I started to bring them together all the time. When President Obama came to visit us [in Sweden], I got to curate part of his visit around innovation and tech. But when I was networking, I wasn't thinking about what they could do for me—I was always trying to help people."

When she invited a younger member of the royal family to lunch at the American embassy by text, which didn't follow official protocols, a "hoopla" ensued. But she stresses that though her methods drove people crazy for a while, gradually they came to the conclusion that "something magical is happening in this embassy. There's an energy again. There are young people coming and artists and immigrant kids."

She took her openness and transparency online into everything she did. A lot of people, including me at one point, worried that it looked too self-promotional. But Natalia says she was just trying to show people "this is what we do every day." That is, host everyone from the king to underprivileged kids from immigrant neighborhoods.

She heard a lot of negative feedback: "I was accused of

having a feminist agenda—in the most gender-equal country in the world. This is the land that founded Skype and Spotify and Minecraft. After a while, people realized that I was an asset, but it took a lot of pushing. And I think if I didn't have this millennial mentality—I don't have to wait my turn; why would I? I wouldn't have accomplished much."

Trying to stay involved once she had a baby, she started a blog called *Millennial Perspective*, for which she did a great deal of research.

As she recalls: "Then—again, I think this is a bit millennial, you don't think about titles or protocol—I just started inviting people over like top CEOs and founders to our residence. I was getting to know people in every company, every start-up, every nonprofit. And I was relating to them around values."

But it wasn't that Natalia wanted to do things her way or to bask in the limelight of her role. It was something more profound. She saw something other people didn't see. As a millennial, she saw the power of breaking down bureaucratic rules and opening the door for a new wave of connectedness.

"They really want to put you in a box. They say, 'Wait, wait, what do you do? What are you? Are you a journalist? Are you a mother? Are you a wife?'

"No, I'm all over the place, and that's the new world. So many people I work with can flow between worlds, between sectors. They're connectors, they're rainmakers, which is a really important role. The thing in today's economy and especially in politics, is bringing people together, especially from different countries. We're really activating a global community of like-minded people and founders, and people who are not afraid to challenge the status quo."

This kind of barely controlled chaos is terrifying to some in older generations; but to millennials like my sister-in-law, "It's fun and dynamic and exciting. It's a new workplace and new economy if millennials can connect that human part. And I think they will."

Natalia's goal of bringing people together in the name of technology, creativity, and collaboration was soon seen as an asset in Sweden, a state that is known for its innovation. She started a movement based on creative collaboration, connectedness, and social media called Brilliant Minds. Natalia is the CEO.

Its own millennial Davos, Brilliant Minds was born from the very work Natalia did as first lady to the American ambassador to Sweden—work that caused so many raised eyebrows.

She explains: "As a platform, we hope to use technology to connect the young leaders of tomorrow.... We believe many of these leaders will emanate from the creative and entrepreneurial communities, because these are communities who are focused on knocking down barriers, fearlessly challenging the status quo and using innovation to make the world different, better, and more connected on every level.

"We can all learn from each other—artists learn from tech, founders learn from artists and musicians, and competitors sit together onstage and around tables debating not the future of their own company or commercial gain, but the future of entire industries and societies."

Natalia's ability to be a connector and to bring people together for a greater cause is now what makes her so successful; it's why people from different industries seek her out. Living in a digital age and using her platform as a millennial, with all the traits that come with it, proved to be incredibly powerful.

The accessibility of tools and resources that allow you to connect broadly are more readily available than ever. That is the reality. In fact, your generation does it better than anyone else.

My sister-in-law Natalia has been able to leverage her social media savviness and digital knowledge to a new level, in ways I frankly did not know were possible. I am now taking a page out of her book! She has inspired me to use social media platforms to grow my own brand and allow followers into some aspects of my personal life. I would never have imagined taking a selfie and posting it from my home, but I have found this level of access resonates with people who follow me. Being both professional AND relatable helps me in the workplace.

Being from a different generation, I've had to learn from these young, brave, tech-savvy women. They're letting their voices be heard, advocating for themselves, and building their brands effectively. And we can all learn a little from that.

CHAPTER TEN

THE WAY FORWARD

When I started writing this book, I wanted to explore with an open mind the challenges young women face in the workplace. And with my coauthor, Daniela, I wanted to give young readers practical advice on what's worked for women who've gotten ahead.

What I found by the book's end was a strong sense of hope, inspired by the future generation of women at work. Young women are making incredible strides in the workplace, gaining on issues like gender pay equity and measures to eradicate sexual harassment in the workplace. Coming of age in the workplace in the #MeToo era, millennials will be more aware of and likely to object to sexual harassment. Between 2012 and 2016, millennials filed 40 percent of the near-25,000 Equal Employment Opportunity Commission (EEOC) sexual harassment charges, which means they filed disproportionately more sexual harassment charges compared to their share of the workforce.

It's so exciting to see women make progress on these issues. In the past eight years, since my first *Knowing Your Value* book debuted, women have been speaking out loudly and demanding to be heard. Things are slowly changing for the next generation.

Just look at the work Boston, Massachusetts, has done to try to narrow the gender pay gap with the recent enactment of the Massachusetts Equal Pay Act, which adds protections for employees against wage discrimination based on gender. It holds employers liable for making sure they are being fair and equal with employees of different genders doing comparable work. The city even set up a special council, the Boston Women's Workforce Council, to team up with organizations and businesses like Morgan Stanley and MIT to help advance the negotiation power of Boston women and offer workshops on topics like salary negotiation.

I love the work that they are doing! It absolutely makes sense. Although the pay gap has narrowed (Pew Research finds that as of 2017, in the U.S., women aged 25 to 34 make 89 cents for every dollar a man of the same age earned), on average women still only earn 82 percent of what a man earns. We NEED more initiatives like those of Boston to continue narrowing that gap. And we are already seeing more organizations and companies invest in tools and resources to level the playing field for women. I am incredibly hopeful that young women entering the workplace will see an end to the pay gap in their lifetime.

There has never been a more opportune time for women in the workplace!

The New World of Work

What started as a quest to try to fill in the gaps about what young women could do to navigate the workplace effectively—and

learn from those who've walked in their shoes before them—
also ended up being a lesson for me.

**This is an exciting time. Although uncharted waters can be
intimidating, it's comforting to know that there is a sea of both
women and men navigating them with you.**

The reality is that in this new world of work, nothing can
be taken for granted. Old ways of doing things simply are not
enough on their own. In the shift that comes with new media
and an ever-changing workplace, job titles come and go. It is
not lost on me that over the course of writing this book, several
women in leadership roles have moved out of them, and then
found new avenues of development and career growth. This is an
exciting time. Although uncharted waters can be intimidating,
it's comforting to know that there is a sea of both women and
men navigating them with you.

As Danielle Weisberg, cofounder of theSkimm, expressed in
earlier chapters, the corporate workplace environment is evolving
rapidly. For her, in some ways, it was less of a risk to go out and
become her own boss, because she had a stronger sense of control
of her destiny. Point being—your way to make your mark on the
world is no longer defined by staying in old lanes. Women like
Anjali Sud of Vimeo have charted their course by taking strategic
risks—switching lanes and moving up the corporate ladder by
making nonlinear career choices. Anjali is a great example of someone charting her own professional journey while understanding the
playing field and navigating her work environment successfully.

Building Resilience

Throughout this book I hope you've learned the significance of digging deep—discovering who you are, the value you bring to the world, and building resilience throughout your career.

For many women, defining your purpose or your passion will not be clear right away—not even close.

Those building-block years will prove to be especially important for gaining self-awareness and a true sense of purpose. You earn the right to do purposeful work by working really hard, observing workplace etiquette, and learning the nuances of your environment in order to get to where you ultimately need to be. Knowing your audience, taking the time to look inward, working on your professional demeanor, and perhaps taking jobs you might not be thrilled about at first can prove important and effective for your professional growth.

Those building-block years will prove to be especially important for gaining self-awareness and a true sense of purpose.

That is why tough moments of feeling downtrodden and stuck, when you wonder why your career isn't moving, are important. You need to listen to these moments and focus inwardly on how to get through them. How will these challenging moments ultimately make you stronger and more resilient? How will they will build your strength and your voice by acknowledging, and then articulating, how a hard-learned lesson at work can be beneficial? That process starts the moment you walk into an office.

So those first trial-and-error years will help you shape that inner compass and polish that inner voice. These formative years will show you how to listen to those gut feelings articulated many times by the women in this book. Take that time to listen. Put down that phone!

Maybe you are the type of young professional who approaches your career with laser vision: You know what you want to do from the start. There are plenty of those examples here, too. André Leon Talley always knew he wanted to be a fashion editor; Emily Jane Fox always wanted to be a journalist; and I knew I wouldn't be happier anywhere but in television. Even then, at the beginning of our careers, we all had to take jobs that were, perhaps, more of a means to an end. We had to work really hard to get in the door, and then put in the hours doing jobs no one else wanted. We polished our professional brands, owning what we brought to the table and communicating it effectively. That was how we got to where we are now.

These are what the building-blocks years are for; you've got to earn your way!

As you've read, it wasn't a straight path for me. I went through my fair share of twists and turns in my career, including being fired, feeling like I was losing everything I had built, and starting all over again. But I dug deep and found new ways to grow my value, which I wouldn't have been able to do if I hadn't hit rock bottom. But it got me to where I am, to the job I love as cohost of *Morning Joe* and the incredible platform I have created around Know Your Value. I've discovered my true calling: helping other women know and grow their personal and professional value, and how to communicate it effectively.

Force yourself to embrace what might be difficult professional years. You may be dealing with a tough boss, having trouble finding your voice, or just feeling adrift. Go through the pointers we outlined and really work to see the "why" behind them. Does your professional demeanor need brushing up? Could you be more effective by using the physical tools we described in chapter three? What's holding you back from effectively advocating for what you bring to the table?

Using Your Voice

Take advantage of mentors, advisors, and people close to you who can help you navigate decisions and choices—but there is no substitute for your inner voice. You are your own best advocate. What I've learned throughout my career and working with women is that we are the worst at acknowledging and acting on that. We hate it! We do it well for anyone but ourselves. But your generation can change that. You have the power to change the course of the workplace, one strong negotiation at a time, as you build your value.

Having a strong sense of self will guide you through times when you doubt yourself, and ultimately help you to achieve your professional goals.

To build your confidence, you need to learn to speak out in real time and push yourself out of your comfort zone. Yes, there are rules and best practices, much of which we've outlined in this book, but there is no substitute for recognizing the professional value you bring to a workplace, and how you communicate it. And THAT you've got to do FROM THE GET-GO.

So get cracking on getting to know your value, and monitor yourself to make sure that when the time is right, you are speaking out and reaching for the opportunities to help you continue to grow. Remember—no one knows what you are thinking if you don't say it!

Put Yourself Out There

To make change, or to make something happen for yourself, you need to get comfortable with putting yourself out there. One of the things I am most proud of in seeing the Know Your Value movement grow is the number of women who have put themselves on the line to communicate their values and advocate for themselves in the moment. Like the moment Daniela pitched her idea on that plane: that's the reason she's helping me write this book!

I predicate my conferences around this notion. In the bonus competition, three women chosen beforehand are groomed and coached. Then they have to get up on stage in a room full of strangers to pitch their value in one minute or less. It's exhilarating to watch these women grow in real time.

A perfect example of the magic that happens when you put yourself on the line can best be exemplified by Jennifer Hotchkiss, a 28-year-old single mom who was a contestant at my first Know Your Value conference in Hartford, Connecticut. Along with the other finalists, she had sixty seconds to get up onstage and pitch why she should be given the grand prize of $10,000. She spoke about her need and deep desire to attend Bay Path University. She spoke with conviction about her desire to be the first one from her family to graduate college, to build a future for her and her family. She found a platform, the Know Your Value competition, and then worked relentlessly to communicate her cause. She really put herself out there.

Jennifer didn't win the contest, but she was a runner-up.

Seeing Jennifer's passion and commitment and sacrifices she had made to succeed even though she didn't win the competition left me convinced that I was going to hire her. I didn't know for what—but I knew that I wanted her on the team, because of her hustle, her strength, and her commitment to advocate for herself.

As I wrapped up the competition, I felt a tug at my leg; a woman in the audience was trying to get my attention. Part of me freaked out, wondering if security was going to step in. She was forceful in demanding that I give her the microphone. Without knowing what was coming next, I handed her the mic.

Nothing would have prepared me to hear the words that came next.

"I'm Caron Hobin, Bay Path's chief strategy officer. We didn't even know that you were going to be part of this today. We were so impressed today with your spunk and your scrappiness, and we want to offer you a scholarship to Bay Path University!"

The emotion in that room was un-replicable. One minute this young woman who had given her all to show her value wasn't even sure if she'd ever get to go to college. But she got up on that stage that day, she put herself out there, and she communicated her value perfectly. Two years later she received her Bachelor of Arts degree in Leadership and Organizational Studies.

And THAT is my primal Know Your Value scream. If you don't put yourself out there, you will NEVER know what could happen. Put yourself out there so things can happen!

Embrace Your Ambition but Work on Your Building Blocks

Once you are in a place where you have honed your skills and have learned and absorbed everything from your workplace—the good AND the bad!—you might even decide to go out on your own. It isn't for everyone, but you might find out that it could be for you. You've got to find the right way to do it. It's a process! Learning the building blocks of business first in a professional workplace can help you get there. If you can communicate effectively what you bring to the table and articulate it with all the physical, emotional, and mental tools we have outlined in this book, there is no stopping you.

Your generation is composed of women from all parts of the country, with diverse life experiences. People like my coauthor, Daniela, who have had to figure things out on their own earlier on and had more to lose if they did not get it right the first time, tend to develop their professional personas at a faster clip. She is a great example of a fearless, ambitious millennial woman who is not apologetic about reaching her goals.

These are the women who will change the workplace for generations to come. Hardworking, tough, determined women, like my sister-in-law, Natalia, who perhaps do things unconventionally, work to leverage technology strategically to create better opportunities to connect and exchange ideas. Women who are making the changes they want to see for themselves, taking charge of their destiny, and turning each hard-learned lesson into resilience and strength.

Embrace Your Inner Leader

One of the best things about millennials and Gen Z is that you won't settle for anything but great leadership. We've seen that if you're not getting it from the traditional workforce, you're out there finding ways to find it.

Cathy Engelbert, CEO of Deloitte, echoes this sentiment about the younger generations: "They are looking for very authentic leaders who will share their stories and bring things to life. I spend a lot of time talking with our people about well-being. You don't have to be superhuman to get to the top.

"There's no doubt that our young professionals are looking for leadership; they're looking for transparency in a way no other generation has.... They're looking for leaders to take the friction out of their daily lives at work, and help them balance it, and help them feel good about what they're doing, their value, and their purpose."

That purpose-driven mentality should be used to fuel the next leaders—and it is all of you! You've seen what works and what doesn't, and can change the face of leadership for generations to come.

Leadership expert Simon Sinek argues that there is a currently "a conspicuous absence in good leadership training in companies today."

Instead of teaching good leadership, Sinek argues, companies largely teach management. "How can we expect people to be good leaders if we don't teach them leadership? I think the responsibility falls very heavily on companies to implement robust training—things like listening skills, communications skills, how to have confrontation, how to give feedback, how to receive feedback, new techniques for incentivizing behavior. I'm tired of listening to executives from companies telling me they incentivize performance. There's no such thing as incentivizing performance. You can only incentivize behavior. What's happening is we're incentivizing behaviors that are bad for people."

But there are things young people in the workforce can do about this, he adds: "The employees themselves also need to become students of leadership. There's a lot of self-work to be done in every generation to find out what our own strengths and weaknesses are. I think this young generation needs to do some heavy self-work on learning how to engage, learning how to have coping skills, how to deal with stress, listening skills, communication skills. I think this generation, like all generations, has some heavy lifting to do themselves. They can't simply fold their arms and be victims of the system they enter. I think patience is an important part of this as well. All of these things take time."

The importance your generation places on good leadership, a socially conscious way of conducting business, an openness and need for diversity and inclusion, and, most important, women's equality in the workplace: all this makes me so hopeful for the future. We need you!

Company and employee models will change, and the way the workplace operates will evolve. Yours is a professional journey ripe with opportunity. Be the leaders you wish to see, earn your right to be one, and then pass the torch and empower others.

Go out there, use these tools, and chart your course. You've got this!

INDEX

257

millennials *(cont.)*
  effect of social media on, 104–105
  electronic communication for, 110
  emotional fluency for, 65, 102–103
  phone dependence for, 94–95
  professional resources for, 5
  promotions for, 161
  purpose-driven work for, 185–187
  risk taking by, 89
  system disruption by, 77–79
Milly, 214
Minecraft, 240
Minkoff, Rebecca, 64–65, 121–122, 175, 214
mistakes, making, 224
MIT (Massachusetts Institute of Technology), 104, 244
mobile technology, 93–102
Mode magazine, 82
Morgan Stanley, 06, 46, 114, 244
Morning Joe (television program), xiii, xx, 1–3, 13, 36, 56, 58, 105–106, 118, 151–152, 171, 191, 235, 247
MSNBC, 13
MTV Networks, 11, 12, 52

N

NACE Salary Calculator, 153
National Partnership for Women & Families, 150
National Science Foundation, 27
naysayers, entrepreneurs and, 220–221
NBC News, 217, 218
NBCUniversal, 2, 10, 14, 37, 38, 56, 89, 155, 161, 219, 227
negative environments, 181–183
networking
  by entrepreneurs, 218–219, 230, 235
  to get your foot in the door, 34–36
  via social media, 237–240
New York Times, 123
Newport, Cal
  on developing a craft, 76–77
  on in-person communication, 104–105
  on job-hopping, 74
  on self-awareness in interviews, 54–55, 58

on social media, 97–98
9/11 terrorist attacks, 187
"no," saying, 175–176
Nordstrom, 233
note-taking, 94–95

O

Obama, Barack, and administration, 6, 13, 84, 237, 239
Occupational Outlook Handbook, 153
Ogilvy, 89
Ohio State University, 27
O*NET OnLine, 153
online presence, 62–63, 131
openness, 113–114, 239
opportunities for career growth
  advocating for yourself regarding, 165–166
  and entrepreneurship, 234
  identifying, 183–184
  leveraging, 191–192
organizations, for networking, 35
out-of-office socializing, 145–147

P

parental engagement, 31–33, 89
Park, Jane, 236
  on asking for promotions, 162
  on changing careers, 195–196
  on compensation negotiations, 158–159
  on empowerment, 225–226
  on entrepreneurship, 221–226
  on making mistakes, 224
  on personalizing business decisions, 224–225
  on teamwork, 124
Parker, Sarah Jessica, 212–217
passion
  of entrepreneurs, 212
  and finding your purpose, 202
  following your, 74–75, 234, 235
pay, asking questions about, 44–45
Payscale.com, 153
peer relationships, 164–165
Penn State, xvii

Williamstown Theater Festival, 21–22
willpower, 9
With Love from Kat blog, 230–231
women. *See also* millennial women;
    young women
    confidence of, in early careers, 129–
        130
    failure/rejection for, 135
    importance of communication for, x
    impulse of, to accommodate, 117–
        118
    missed cues for, 147
    and others' expectations, 192
    in STEM fields, 26–29
    traditional workplace as viewed by,
        166–167
work ethic, 84–85
workplace
    challenges for young women in, xi–
        xii, 26–34
    current, 244–245
    support in, xviii
    traditional, women's views of, 166–
        167
    warmth and support in, 33–34
"worst-case scenario" thinking, 195–199

Y

"yes," saying, 87–88, 174–178
young professionals. *See also* millennials
    promotions for, 159–161
    value of entry-level jobs for, 77–79
young women
    ambition for, 9–10, 120–125
    anxiety of, about career path, 72
    career growth for, 173
    confidence of, 130–131
    corporate connections for, 228–229
    entrepreneurship for, 210–211
    feedback for, 114–115
    gender wage gap for, 150–151
    millennial midlife crisis for, 170–171
    speaking up by, 111
    traditional workplace as viewed by,
        166–167
    work-related values of, 174–175
    workplace challenges for, xi–xii, 26–
        34

Z

Zakin, Carly, 217–220

266